❧ Charles Dickens ❧
c. 1859

The
DICKENS
Family Gospel

DICKENS

by Robert C. Hanna

LEGACY PRESS
A Division of Rainbow Publishers

All scripture verses unless otherwise indicated are taken from the
King James Version of the Bible.

THE DICKENS FAMILY GOSPEL
by Robert Hanna
ISBN 1-885358-36-9
©1998 by Legacy Press

Legacy Press
P.O. Box 261129
San Diego, CA 92196

Illustrator: Terry J. Walderhaug
Editor: Christy Allen
Design: Stray Cat Studio, San Diego, CA

Photos on cover and page one reproduced
courtesy of the Dickens House Museum, London.

⁀ Acknowledgments ⁀

The concept for this book originated with Dr. Elliot Engel of North Carolina State University. Christy Allen, editor at Legacy Press, provided invaluable suggestions which enabled me to achieve the complete set of thirty-two study guides. Lesley H. Hanna, my wife, consistently offered encouragement and support, without which I could not have prepared this book. Finally, I dedicate *The Dickens Family Gospel* to my two daughters, Charlotte Hanna and Emily Hanna, to whom I repeat Charles Dickens' own words: "I most strongly and affectionately impress upon you the priceless value of the New Testament, and the study of that Book as the one unfailing guide in life."

Contents

Foreword

Undoubtedly, Charles Dickens would be gratified that his book *A Christmas Carol* remains such an astounding success more than 100 years after his death in 1870. And yet surprisingly, this great author—so closely associated with Christmas— is not generally known for his role as a teacher of Christianity. Dickens' family Gospel, written for the novelist's own children in 1846, is not nearly as well-known as the names of Dickens' fictional children—Tiny Tim, Oliver Twist, the Artful Dodger, Little Nell, Pip, and Estella, to name just a few.

But, now, Robert C. Hanna's marvelous book, which uniquely focuses on Dickens' religious education for his own nine children, should do much to add to our understanding of Dickens as a Christian parent and teacher. Dr. Hanna is the first to explore Dickens' sincere and lifelong interest in both children and their Christian education. By devising interactive Christian education study guides, he brilliantly revives Charles Dickens' own noble accomplishment of making Jesus' words the foundation for children's moral education. And thanks to Dr. Hanna's work, thousands of children Dickens could never meet will benefit from Dickens' portrayal of the teachings of Christ.

I suspect that Mr. Dickens would view rather skeptically the hundreds of academic books and articles on his novels which are regularly published each year. (Many trace obscure themes or stress themes that might be of interest only to English professors.) But I am convinced that Dickens would be both grateful and delighted with Robert C. Hanna's excellent work, *The Dickens Family Gospel.* I know that I am.

— Dr. Elliot D. Engel
Professor, North Carolina State University
and Leading Authority on Charles Dickens

⌦ Preface ⌫

I can never write about Charles Dickens without fondly remembering my mother's request when I started high school, in 1966, that I borrow a copy of *Oliver Twist* from the school's library. That she, an avid reader, could have sooner borrowed a copy from the public library or purchased a copy from our town's bookstore seems not to have occurred to me. That the novel was for her reading pleasure was never in doubt, until I handed it to her. She gave me a puzzled look and handed it right back, saying that it was for me to read. She had already read it. So began my lifetime interest in the works and life of Dickens, leading thirty years later to my preparation of this original curricular edition of his little known family Gospel.

Dickens' family Gospel, on which these lessons are based, is unlike anything else that he ever wrote. It is his sole curricular work, and he taught it only in his own household and only to his own nine children. From its composition in 1846 until Dickens' death in 1870, the author never gave the work a formal title, referring to it once in a letter as a children's New Testament.

When Dickens' youngest child, Edward, left home in 1868 to join a brother in Australia, Dickens presented him with a New Testament and a letter of fatherly advice. He wrote:

"I put a New Testament among your books for the very same reasons and with the very same hopes that made me write an easy account of it for you, when you were a little child; because it is the best book that ever was or will be known in the world, and because it teaches you the best lessons by which any human creature who tries to be truthful and faithful to duty can possibly be guided."

The "easy account of it" was finally published in 1934 as *The Life of Our Lord*, and the work has appeared in over forty editions worldwide. What makes *The Dickens Family Gospel* edition unique is its abridgment of the original text into thirty-two study guides, supplemented with small group activities and illustrative excerpts from other writings by Dickens. The result is an interactive Christian education curriculum which goes beyond merely advising adults to read *The Life of Our Lord* aloud to children. Numerous opportunities are provided to recapture the group spirit of Dickens' Christian instruction in his own household, during both the readings and the activities.

Throughout the study guides, I have generally modernized Dickens' spelling and punctuation. I have also corrected minor errors contained in *The Life of Our Lord*, just as Dickens surely would have done during his readings and discussions. He never formally edited the text for publication.

— Robert C. Hanna
Hillsdale, Michigan

⌒ How to Use This Book ⌒

Charles Dickens simplified parts of the Gospels and the book of Acts for three significant reasons. First, he wanted his children to comprehend and manifest moral behavior, based on the teachings of Jesus, at an earlier age than the language of the King James Version of the New Testament could be expected to promote. Second, he wanted Christian education to occur in community "where two or three are gathered together in My name." Third, he wanted Jesus' teachings to be heard, just as Jesus spoke aloud whenever He taught. Accordingly, it is essential that the principles of understandable vocabulary, learning in community, and oral presentation be adhered to when implementing these study guides. Any instructional approach which alters these three principles will seriously compromise the teaching methods which Charles Dickens found most effective with his children for nearly a quarter of a century.

Each lesson contains four sections: text from *The Life of Our Lord*, an excerpt from Dickens' other writings which complements the New Testament text, an activity, and a suggested prayer. These latter sections, while not essential to teaching from the New Testament, help recreate the learning environment of the Dickens household. Although Dickens' son Alfred tells us that his father's way with words was not limited to his writings, it is to his writings alone that we can now turn for lessons and themes which complement his simplified New Testament. Daughter Mamie tells us that her father would give prizes for excellent school work and that "a word of commendation from him was indeed most highly cherished, and would set our hearts glowing with pride and pleasure." Activities with a Christian focus under adult leadership can promote pride and pleasure as well.

Another advantage to having four sections per lesson is flexibility. For instance, in a home schooling setting, a parent who shares a passage orally with a daughter or son will already experience a close relationship and so may forego some of the activities. The content of the text and the companion passage can stand alone. Similarly, in a weekly church school setting, a teacher who shares a passage orally with a small group may not always have time to add the excerpt from Dickens' other writings. The text and the activity can nonetheless suffice. Additional instructional opportunity results from the wealth of Gospel content which Dickens drew upon from the King James Bible. The books, chapters, and verses which Dickens consulted in the New Testament are always identified after each passage from *The Life of Our Lord,* allowing the parent or teacher to look up the original text and then compare the two versions, or to access New Testament content located immediately before or after Dickens' excerpts. All source identification is taken from *Telling "The Blessed History": Charles Dickens's "The Life of Our Lord"* by Madonna Egan. Each activity is intentionally written in a narrative format. When Dickens joined his children to read and discuss his children's New Testament, he did not rely upon a formal lesson plan with designated minutes for time on task. Rather, he came to his children with his life experiences (of which his literature played no small part) and his simplified Gospel. It was his desire and expectation that his children develop a consciousness of caring, service and love through an intimate knowledge and understanding of the New Testament, what he called "the one unfailing guide in life."

Finally, children should be permitted to interrupt a reading, ask questions, make comments, and respond to Jesus' teachings. Even with Dickens' care in selecting and rewriting New Testament passages, there will still be words and concepts that some children will not understand or about which they will want to know more. A case study which illustrates this point, based on sharing this material with my daughter, Emily, is found in an appendix to this edition. Just as the teaching effectiveness of Dickens' manuscript depended on the presence and patience of a father among his children, so does the teaching effectiveness of these thirty-two study guides depend on the presence and patience of the adult. As Charles Dickens well knew, it is always important to listen to children as they come to know Jesus as their Lord and Savior.

Note: Beginning with Lesson Seven, the parent or teacher will frequently use a "Lot Box" during the activities. A simply decorated box or basket may serve as an effective Lot Box, and will become recognizable to the children as a special part of the learning activity.

The Importance of Knowing Jesus

• Activity •

Give each child an index card and a marker and ask the children to print their names and decorate their cards. Display the finished name cards on a wall or bulletin board.

Ask, **Do you know why you were given your name?** Allow everyone to respond. Children in a class setting who do not know each other well will begin to learn about each other's families.

Continue by asking, **Do you know what your name means?** Consult a directory of names for their names' meanings. Expect additional comments in favor of or against the book's explanations.

If no one is named Charles, ask, **What do you think the name "Charles" means?** Look up the name and read its meaning to the children.

Then ask, **What do you think the name "Scrooge" means?** Expect some accurate answers—the characters and story of Dickens' *A Christmas Carol* are familiar to most children. Encourage them to tell what they know about the story (memories will be based on different versions, from live performances to movies to family readings). Show that the name "Scrooge" is not in the book of names, but that it is found in a large dictionary.

Ask, **What needs to happen in order for a new word to be added to a dictionary?**

Say, **Charles Dickens wrote *A Christmas Carol.* He also wrote *The Life of Our Lord,* a book about Jesus and His teachings. How would Dickens or anyone else begin a book about Jesus and His teachings?**

• The Life of Our Lord •

My dear children, I am very anxious that you should know something about the history of Jesus Christ. For everybody ought to know about Him. No one ever lived who was so good, so kind, so gentle, and so sorry for all people who did wrong or were in any way ill or miserable, as He was. And as He is now in heaven, where we hope to go, and all to meet each other after we are dead, and there be happy always together, you never can think what a good place heaven is, without knowing who He was and what He did.

Ask, **Why would Charles Dickens want his children to know about Jesus and heaven?**

• Another Thought •

From a letter written by Charles Dickens to his youngest son, Edward, who was leaving home for Australia:

I put a New Testament among your books for the very same reasons and with the very same hopes that made me write an easy account of it for you, when you were a little child; because it is the best book that ever was or will be known in the world, and because it teaches you the best lessons by which any human creature who tries to be truthful and faithful to duty can possibly be guided. As your brothers have gone away, one by one, I have written to each such words as I am now writing to you, and have entreated them all to guide themselves by this book, putting aside the interpretations and inventions of man.

You will remember that you have never at home been harassed about religious observances or mere formalities. I have always been anxious not to weary my children with such things before they are old enough to form opinions respecting them. You will therefore understand the better that I now most solemnly impress upon you the truth and beauty of the Christian religion, as it came from Christ Himself, and the impossibility of your going far wrong if you humbly but heartily respect it.

Only one thing more on this head. The more we are in earnest as to feeling it, the less we are disposed to hold forth about it. Never abandon the wholesome practice of saying your own private prayers night and morning. I have never abandoned it myself, and I know the comfort of it.

I hope you will always be able to say in after life that you had a kind father. You cannot show your affection for him so well or make him so happy as by doing your duty.

— Your affectionate Father

Charles Dickens uses the word "duty" twice in this letter, once in the context of duty to God and once in the context of duty to a parent. Ask, **What does "duty" mean? How is "duty" the same with God and your parents? How is "duty" unique when we think of God as our Parent?**

• Prayer •

God, help us to be eager to learn more about you. We should remember that it is our duty as Your children to worship You and know You. Thank You for loving us. Amen.

‍ Jesus' Birth ‍

• Activity •

Provide the children with drawing paper and colored pencils. Say, **Draw a picture of where you were born. Use your imagination!** If the children do not know what their place of birth looks like, encourage them to draw what they think it might look like.

• The Life of Our Lord •

[Jesus] was born a long, long time ago—nearly two thousand years ago—at a place called Bethlehem. His father and mother lived in a city called Nazareth, but they were forced by business to travel to Bethlehem. His father's name was Joseph, and his mother's name was Mary. And the town being very full of people, also brought there by business, there was no room for Joseph and Mary in the inn or in any house; so they went into a stable to lodge, and in this stable Jesus Christ was born. There was no cradle or anything of that kind there, so Mary laid her pretty little boy in what is called the manger, which is the place the horses eat out of, and there He fell asleep. [Text: Luke 2:1-7]

Ask, **Do you think Jesus would remember the stable in which He was born or the manger in which He was placed? How might He know about these, even though He was a baby when He was in the manger in the stable?** Provide time for each child to tell about his or her picture. If a picture includes someone in a room or next to a building, ask the child how he or she knows who was there. Ask, **Do we have to remember something in**

order for it to be true? **Do we have to be where something happened in order for it to be true?** Display the pictures on a wall or bulletin board, next to the children's names from Lesson One.

• Another Thought •

Charles Dickens wrote many books in addition to *The Life of Our Lord* and *A Christmas Carol.* One of his first books was *Oliver Twist.* He began this book by telling about Oliver's birth:

What an excellent example of the power of dress young Oliver Twist was! Wrapped in the blanket which had hitherto formed his only covering, he might have been the child of a nobleman or a beggar; it would have been hard for the haughtiest stranger to have assigned him his proper station in society. But now that he was enveloped in the old calico robes which had grown yellow in the same service, he was badged and ticketed, and fell into his place at once—a parish child—the orphan of a workhouse...

Discuss whether Dickens is correct when he suggests that we cannot tell if a baby belongs to a poor family or a well-to-do family, just by seeing it wrapped in a blanket. Ask, **Was Jesus born to a poor family or a well-to-do family? How do you know? Was God present at Jesus' birth? Is God present at everyone's birth? What does this tell us about God as a Parent?**

• Prayer •

God, thank You for always being with us, just as You were for baby Jesus' birth and for our births. We are glad that You love us and take care of us, regardless of who we are.

⋍ Giving to Others ⋍

• Activity •

Play an alphabet game by having the children name gifts that one person could give to another. The first child should name a gift that begins with the letter A, then the next child names a gift that starts with the letter B, and so on. List the gifts on a poster board or a large sheet of paper. When the alphabet is complete, ask, **Can any of the gifts be given by anyone, anytime, without cost?** Circle the gifts that fit the criteria, as the children select them. Examples include: affection, a blessing, encouragement, a hug, love and a smile. (If there are no such gifts on the list, play more of the alphabet game until several responses which fit the criteria are given.)

Next, give each child an index card and a pencil, and have each child write on the index card the name of one gift which cannot be purchased but that can always be given. Then have the children cover their cards with gift wrap and attach a gift tag for the family member whom they select to surprise with the gift later.

• The Life of Our Lord •

Now the great place of all that country was Jerusalem—just as London is the great place in England—and at Jerusalem the king lived, whose name was King Herod. Some wise men came one day from a country a long way off in the East, and said to the king, "We have seen a star in the sky, which teaches us to know that a child is born in Bethlehem who will live to be a man whom all people will love." When King Herod heard this, he was jealous, for he was a wicked man. But he pretended not to be, and said to the wise men, "Whereabouts is this child?" And the wise men said, "We don't know. But we think the star will show us; for the star has been moving on before us, all the way here, and is now standing still in the sky." Then Herod asked them to see if the star would show them where the child lived, and ordered them, if they found the child, to come back to him. So they went out, and the star went on, over their heads a little way before them, until it stopped over the house where the child was. This was very wonderful, but God ordered it to be so.

When the star stopped, the wise men went in and saw the child with Mary, His mother. They loved Him very much, and gave Him some presents. Then they went away. But they did not go back to King Herod, for they thought he was jealous, though he had not said so. So they went away, by night, back into their own country. And an angel came and told Joseph and Mary to take the child into a country called Egypt, or Herod would kill Him. So they escaped, too, in the night—the father, the mother, and the child—and arrived there safely. [Text: Matthew 2:1-14]

Ask, **What gifts would you have given baby Jesus if you had been there with Him? How can we still give presents to Jesus today?**

• Another Thought •

Charles Dickens wrote in *A Christmas Carol:*
Running to the window, [Scrooge] opened it, and put out his head…

"What's today?" cried Scrooge, calling downward to a boy in Sunday clothes, who perhaps had loitered in to look about him. "Eh?" returned the boy, with all his might of wonder.

"What's today, my fine fellow?" said Scrooge.

"Today!" replied the boy. "Why, CHRISTMAS DAY."

"It's Christmas Day!" said Scrooge to himself. "I haven't missed it. The Spirits have done it all in one night. They can do anything they like. Of course they can. Of course they can. Hallo, my fine fellow!"

"Hallo!" returned the boy.

"Do you know the poulterer's, in the next street but one at the corner?" Scrooge inquired.

"I should hope I did," replied the lad.

"An intelligent boy!" said Scrooge. "A remarkable boy! Do you know whether they've sold the prize turkey that was hanging up there? Not the little prize turkey— the big one?"

"What, the one as big as me?" returned the boy.

"What a delightful boy!" said Scrooge. "It's a pleasure to talk to him. Yes, my buck!"

"It's hanging there now," replied the boy.

"Is it?" said Scrooge. "Go and buy it, and tell 'em to bring it here, that I may give them the direction where to take it. Come back with the man, and I'll give you a shilling. Come back with him in less than five minutes and I'll give you half a crown!"

The boy was off like a shot. He must have had a steady hand at a trigger who could have got a shot off half so fast.

"I'll send it to Bob Cratchit's!" whispered Scrooge, rubbing his hands, and splitting with a laugh. "He shan't know who sends it. It's twice the size of Tiny Tim."

Scrooge was better than his word. He did it all, and infinitely more; and to Tiny Tim, who did not die, he was a second father.

Ask, **What present that can be bought did Scrooge give to the Cratchit family? What present that cannot be bought did Scrooge give to the Cratchit family?** Discuss what it means to be a "second father." Review from Lessons One and Two how God is our Father and remind the children that we say so whenever we say the Lord's Prayer. Ask, **What presents that cannot be bought does God give us?**

• Prayer •

God, we are so grateful for all You give us. Help us to be like You and to show Your gifts to other people every day. Amen.

⌒ Overcoming Fear ⌒

• Activity •

Display the word AFRAID in large capital letters on a poster board or a large sheet of paper. Give each child construction paper, a pencil and scissors. Have everyone draw and cut out the letters for AFRAID. Talk about things that we are sometimes afraid of. Ask, **Just because we fear something, does that always mean that what we fear is bad or harmful?** Then tell the children to rearrange the letters and to look for three different three-letter words that say how we can overcome fear of something that God does not want us to fear. Have the children use these words in sentences to explain how God can help us with our fear. (The words to find are "aid," "far" and "rid.") Say, **If we ask, God can aid us when we are afraid, take our fear far away, and rid us of our fear.**

• The Life of Our Lord •

While [Jesus] was asleep, some shepherds who were watching sheep in the fields saw an angel from God, all light and beautiful, come moving over the grass towards them. At first they were afraid and fell down and hid their faces. But it said, "There is a child born today in the city of Bethlehem near here, who will grow up to be so good that God will love Him as His own Son; and He will teach men to love one another, and not to quarrel and hurt one another; and His name will be Jesus Christ; and people will put that name in their prayers, because they will know God loves it, and will know that they should love it, too." And then the angel told the shepherds to go to

that stable and look at that little child in the manger, which they did; and they kneeled down by it in its sleep and said, "God bless this child!" [Text: Luke 2:8-12, 15-16]

Have the children tell what they know about angels. Ask, **If angels are from God and are good, why would the shepherds fear one? Could they have been afraid because they did not know how to behave in front of an angel?** Explain that God did not want the shepherds to be afraid. Instead, He wanted them to listen to His angel. Ask, **What did God's angels tell the shepherds? Why is it important for us to know and tell others about Jesus, too?**

• Another Thought •

Charles Dickens wrote a book titled *Great Expectations.* The narrator is Pip, who, as a child, stole a metal file from his brother-in-law, the blacksmith Joe. Afterwards, Pip explains:

It was much upon my mind (particularly when I first saw him looking about for his file) that I ought to tell Joe the whole truth. Yet I did not, and for the reason that I mistrusted that if I did, he would think me worse than I was. The fear of losing Joe's confidence, and of thenceforth sitting in the chimney-corner at night staring drearily at my forever lost companion and friend, tied up my tongue…. In a word, I was too cowardly to do what I knew to be right, as I had been too cowardly to avoid doing what I knew to be wrong.

Say, **Pip is afraid that Joe will no longer like him or trust him if he tells Joe the truth about the stolen file. What should Pip do? Why? Sometimes we find it difficult to tell the truth when we have done wrong,**

but does God want us to act on our fear and tell a lie, or to overcome our fear and tell the truth? Affirm to the children that the Bible is the Word of God, and that God never lies to us.

• Prayer •

God, sometimes we have fears, but we know that You are always with us. The one thing we should fear is not doing what You have told us is right in the Bible. Help us to turn to You for guidance. Amen.

⌒ Praising God Through Song ⌒

• Activity •

Give each child three index cards and a pencil to record the names of his or her three favorite Christmas carols about Jesus, one on each card. Collect all of the cards and mix them up. Select and read one card at a time. With the help of the children, classify each response as either a Christmas carol about Jesus or not. On a poster board or a large sheet of paper, keep a tally of correct responses, and then rank the correct responses in order of popularity. Ask, **Who might have sung the very first Christmas carols?** Be sure to include everyone who was present at the time surrounding Jesus' birth: Mary and Joseph, the shepherds and the wise men.

Review Lesson Four, in which the angel appeared to the shepherds. Ask, **What three things do we usually associate with drawings of angels?** Answers should include wings, halos, and harps. **Could angels have sung the very first Christmas carols? What musical instrument could have accompanied their singing? Do we have to wait for the season of Christmas in order to praise God by singing Christmas carols? Why is it good to praise God every day?** Lead everyone in singing a verse or two of the children's favorite Christmas carols.

• The Life of Our Lord •

When King Herod was dead, an angel came to Joseph again and said he might now go to Jerusalem, and not be afraid for the child's sake. So Joseph and Mary, and her son Jesus Christ (who are commonly called the Holy Family)

traveled towards Jerusalem, but hearing on the way that King Herod's son was the new king, and fearing that he, too, might want to hurt the child, they turned out of the way and went to live in Nazareth. They lived there until Jesus Christ was twelve years old. [Text: Matthew 2:19-23]

• Another Thought •

Charles Dickens wrote several short stories as well as books. One story is titled *The Seven Poor Travelers,* and in this story seven men share a meal on Christmas Eve. Although they are strangers to each other, they break bread as fellow Christians:

Christmas Eve, my friends, when the shepherds, who were poor travelers, too, in their way, heard the angels sing, "On earth, peace. Goodwill towards men!"

I don't know who was the first among us to think that we ought to take hands as we sat, in deference to the toast, or whether any one of us anticipated the others, but at any rate we all did.

Say, **Let's join hands as the seven poor travelers did, and sing one more Christmas carol for Jesus. Which one should we sing?**

• Prayer •

Thank You, God, for the gift of music. We will always praise You by singing, just as the angels did when Jesus was born. Amen.

☞ The Importance of Prayer: Part One ☜

• Activity •

Distribute index cards and pencils. Ask each child to think of one question to ask about Charles Dickens and to print it on a blank card. Make certain that the children put their names on the cards as well. Collect the cards for use during Lesson Seven and promise to find answers to their questions, but for now provide some general background information about Dickens. Mention that he lived and worked in London in the 1800s, that he was the most popular writer in his day, and that all of his books are still available today.

Tell the children that Dickens experienced poverty as a child and that his father was put in prison for not being able to pay his bills. No matter how famous and wealthy Dickens ever became, he never forgot how important it is for a child to have a good home, good health and a good education. Mention that Dickens had nine children of his own, to whom he often read and talked about the readings the children have been hearing from *The Life of Our Lord*.

• The Life of Our Lord •

Then Joseph and Mary went to Jerusalem to attend a religious feast which used to be held in those days in the Temple of Jerusalem, which was a great church or cathedral, and they took Jesus Christ with them. And when the feast was over, they traveled away from Jerusalem, back towards their own home in Nazareth, with a great many of their friends and neighbors. For people used, then, to

travel a great many together for fear of robbers, the roads not being so safe and well guarded as they are now, and traveling being much more difficult altogether than it now is.

They traveled on, for a whole day, and never knew that Jesus Christ was not with them, for the company being so large, they thought He was somewhere among the people, though they did not see Him. But finding that He was not there, and fearing that He was lost, they turned back to Jerusalem in great anxiety to look for Him. They found Him sitting in the temple, talking about the goodness of God, and how we should all pray to Him, with some learned men who were called doctors. They were not what you understand by the word "doctors" now; they did not attend sick people. They were scholars and clever men. And Jesus Christ showed such knowledge in what He said to them, and in the questions He asked them, that they were all astonished.

He went with Joseph and Mary home to Nazareth, when they had found Him, and lived there until He was thirty or thirty-five years old. [Text: Luke 2:41-47, 51]

Ask, **What does "prayer" mean?**

• Another Thought •

Charles Dickens wrote the following prayer for His children:

Hear what our Lord Jesus Christ taught to His disciples and to us, and what we should remember every day of our lives, to love the Lord our God with all our heart, and with all our mind, and with all our soul, and with all our strength; to love our neighbors as ourselves, to do unto other people as we would have them do unto us, and to be charitable and gentle to all. There is no other commandment, our Lord Jesus Christ said, greater than these.

Ask, **Why would Charles Dickens write a prayer for his children to recite? Where did Dickens find most of the words in this prayer? How do we know? Does God welcome our own original prayers? What does this tell us about God?**

• Prayer •

We are glad that we can talk to You anytime and anywhere. Remind us to talk to You often so we can learn to be more like You. Amen.

Lesson Seven

⋐ Promises: Part One ⋑

• Activity •

Cut several straws into different lengths. Hold them in your hand so that their lengths cannot be determined before each child takes one. Announce that whoever draws the shortest straw will receive a gift copy of *A Christmas Carol.*

After the straws have been selected and the book has been awarded, ask, **What makes drawing straws so fair?** Explain that the practice can be found in biblical times and that it was called drawing "lots." For examples, read aloud from Joshua 18:5-6, Nehemiah 11:1 and Acts 1:24-26.

Introduce the Lot Box, which should contain the questions about Charles Dickens' life from Lesson Six. Draw out the cards and answer the questions, based on a biography of Dickens with an index or any research you have conducted. (Some questions may have already been answered during the activity in Lesson Six.)

Ask, **How would you have felt if I had not kept my promise to find the answers to your questions?** If the children's responses are tolerant and understanding, ask what their feelings would be if no one ever kept any promises made to them. If their responses are critical, ask if it still would have mattered to them if you could have offered them a "good excuse" for not keeping your promise.

• The Life of Our Lord •

At that time there was a very good man indeed, named John, who was the son of a woman named Elizabeth—the cousin of Mary. And people being wicked, and violent, and killing each other, and not minding their duty towards God, John (to teach them better) went about the country, preaching to them and entreating them to be better men and women. And because he loved them more than himself, and didn't mind himself when he was doing them good, he was poorly dressed in the skin of a camel and ate little but some insects called locusts, which he found as he traveled, and wild honey, which the bees left in the hollow trees. You never saw a locust, because they belong to that country near Jerusalem, which is a great way off. So do camels, but I think you have seen a camel. At all events, they are brought over here, sometimes, and if you would like to see one, I will show you one.

There was a river, not very far from Jerusalem, called the River Jordan, and in this water John baptized those people who would come to him and promise to be better. A great many people went to him in crowds. Jesus Christ went, too. But when John saw Him, John said, "Why should I baptize You, who are so much better than I!" Jesus Christ made answer, "Suffer it to be so now." So John baptized Him. And when He was baptized, the sky opened, and a beautiful bird like a dove came flying down, and the voice of God, speaking up in Heaven, was heard to say, "This is My beloved Son, in whom I am well pleased!"

Jesus Christ then went into a wild and lonely country called the Wilderness, and stayed there forty days and forty nights, praying that He might be of use to men and women and teach them to be better, so that after their deaths, they might be happy in Heaven. [Text: Matthew 3:1-6, 13-17 and 4:1-11; Mark 1:2-6, 9-13; Luke 3:1-6, 21-22 and 4:1-13]

Review and discuss the two promises made in this passage:

1. Dickens promised to take his children to see a camel if they asked.

2. People who came to John for baptism promised to lead better lives.

Have the children consider which promise was more important to keep and why. Ask, **Should the less important promise be kept anyway? Why?**

• Another Thought •

Charles Dickens wrote to the Countess of Blessington:

I remember my promise, as in cheerful duty bound, and with Heaven's grace will redeem it. At this moment, I have not the faintest idea how, but I am going into Scotland on the nineteenth to see Jeffrey, and while I am away (I shall return, please God, in about three weeks) will look out for some accident, incident, or subject for small description, to send you when I come home. You will take the will for the deed, I know.

Ask, **Is meaning to keep a promise the same as keeping it?**

Charles Dickens wrote to Douglas Jerrold:

As half a loaf is better than no bread, so I hope that half a sheet of paper may be better than none at all, coming from one who is anxious to live in your memory and friendship. I should have redeemed the pledge I gave you in this regard long since, but occupation at one time, and absence from pen and ink at another, have prevented me.

Ask, **Do you think that keeping a promise late is better than not keeping it at all?**

• Prayer •

God, You keep all of Your promises. We need to be like You and keep our promises, too, especially our promise to follow You. Amen.

⌒ Promises: Part Two ⌒

• Activity •

Distribute construction paper and markers. Have each child write out his or her name and then write a good promise to make and keep, beginning with each letter in his or her name. Let the children replace their decorated names from Lesson One with this variation on their names.

Place each child's name on a slip of paper, draw them from the Lot Box, and then ask each child to explain the importance of three of the promises displayed within someone else's name. Discuss when it would be wrong to keep a promise, such as when doing so would harm someone else. Review John's baptism of Jesus from the excerpt from *The Life of Our Lord* in Lesson Seven. Ask, **Can anyone tell us what happened to John later?**

• The Life of Our Lord •

Now Herod, the son of that cruel king who murdered the innocents, reigning over the people there, and hearing that Jesus Christ was doing these wonders, and was giving sight to the blind and causing the deaf to hear and the dumb to speak and the lame to walk, and that He was followed by multitudes and multitudes of people—Herod, hearing this, said, "This man is a companion and friend of John the Baptist." John was the good man, you recollect, who wore a garment made of camel's hair and ate wild honey. Herod had taken him prisoner, because he taught and preached to the people, and had him then locked up in the prisons of his palace.

While Herod was in this angry humor with John, his birthday came, and his niece, the daughter of Herodias, who was a fine dancer, danced before him to please him. She pleased him so much that he swore an oath he would give her whatever she would ask him for. "Then," said she, "Uncle, give me the head of John the Baptist in a charger." For her mother hated John and was a wicked, cruel woman.

The king was sorry, for though he had John prisoner, he did not wish to kill him; but having sworn that he would give her what she asked for, he sent some soldiers down into the prison with directions to cut off the head of John the Baptist and give it to Herodias' daughter. This they did and took it to her, as she had said, in a charger, which was a kind of dish. When Jesus Christ heard from the apostles of this cruel deed, he left that city and went with them (after they had privately buried John's body in the night) to another place. [Text: Matthew 14:1-13; Mark 6:14-32]

Discuss with the children what Herod's response concerning his promise, or oath, should have been. Praise the children for making good promises which will help, not hurt, others, and ask them each to try to keep one in particular before meeting for Lesson Nine. Review the good which Jesus did in the excerpt above.

• Another Thought •

Charles Dickens wrote to Baroness Burdett-Coutts:
You may possibly have seen a preface I wrote, before leaving England, to a little book by a working man; and may have learned from the newspapers that he is dead: leaving a destitute wife and six children, of whom one is a cripple. I have addressed a letter to the governors of the

Orphan Working School in behalf of the eldest boy: and they tell me he has a good chance of being elected into that institution in April next. It has occurred to me that at some time or other you might have an opportunity of presenting one of the girls to some other school or charity, and as I know full well that in such an event you would rather thank than blame me for making a real and strong case known to you, I send you the children's names and ages.

Amelia Overs	11 years old
John Richard	9
Harriett	7
Geraldine	6
Editha	4
John	4 months

They live, at present, at 55 Vauxhall Street, Lambeth.

Ask, **What good did Charles Dickens try to do for the family in this letter? What specific needs would the mother and her children share?** Consider each family member in turn. **What unique need might a person of each age have? How could persons who are more fortunate help a family like this today?**

• Prayer •

There are many people who need help, God. Use us to help others, especially those who do not know You. Amen.

⌐ Charity ⌐

• Activity •

Use the Lot Box to group the children into pairs.
Distribute construction paper and markers and ask the
partners to list together five things they would both like
to receive as birthday gifts. After the list is prepared, ask
for a new list which contains five things anyone who is
very poor would need right now.

When everyone has finished, replace the birth pictures from Lesson Two with the children's lists. Have the
children tell about the content of the list they compiled
with their partners. Then read aloud to the children all of
the items from the second lists. Ask, **Why are the items
on the two lists so different?** List on a poster board or
a large sheet of paper the children's suggestions for how
they could help someone who is poor obtain the items on
the second list. Display these responses as well.

• The Life of Our Lord •

That there might be some good men to go about
with Him, teaching the people, Jesus Christ chose twelve
poor men to be his companions. These twelve are called
the apostles, or disciples, and He chose them from among
poor men in order that the poor might know always after
that, in all years to come, that Heaven was made for them
as well as for the rich, and that God makes no difference
between those who wear good clothes and those who go
barefoot and in rags. The most miserable, the most ugly,
deformed, wretched creatures who live, will be bright
angels in Heaven if they are good here on earth. Never

forget this when you are grown up. Never be proud or unkind, my dears, to any poor man, woman, or child. If they are bad, think that they would have been better if they had had kind friends and good homes and had been better taught. So, always try to make them better by kind, persuading words, and always try to teach them and relieve them if you can. And when people speak ill of the poor and miserable, think how Jesus Christ went among them and taught them and thought them worthy of His care. And always pity them yourselves and think as well of them as you can....

As [Jesus] was teaching them thus, he sat near the public treasury, where people as they passed along the street were accustomed to drop money into a box for the poor, and many rich persons, passing while Jesus sat there, had put in a great deal of money. At last there came a poor widow who dropped in two mites, each half a farthing in value, and then went quietly away. Jesus, seeing her do this as He rose to leave the place, called His disciples about Him and said to them that that poor widow had been more truly charitable than all the rest who had given money that day, for the others were rich and would never miss what they had given, but she was very poor and had given those two mites which might have bought her bread to eat.

Let us never forget what the poor widow did, when we think we are charitable.[Text: Matthew 10:2-4; Mark 3:14-19 and 12:41-44; and Luke 6:13-16 and 21:1-4]

Ask, **Why did Charles Dickens tell his children never to forget what the poor widow did?** Point out that in addition to giving much, the widow gave quietly and privately. Ask, **Why didn't she make certain that everyone present knew about her contribution?**

• Another Thought •

From Charles Dickens' autobiographical fragment:
It is wonderful to me how I could have been so easily cast away at such an age. It is wonderful to me, that even after my descent into the poor little drudge I had been since we came to London, no one had compassion enough on me—a child of singular abilities, quick, eager, delicate, and soon hurt, bodily or mentally—to suggest that something might have been spared, as certainly it might have been, to place me at any common school…

I was so young and childish, and so little qualified—how could I be otherwise?—to undertake the whole charge of my own existence, that, in going to Hungerfordstairs of a morning, I could not resist the stale pastry put out at half price on trays at the confectioners' doors in Tottenham Court Road; and I often spent in that the money I should have kept for my dinner. Then I went without my dinner, or bought a roll, or a slice of pudding…

I know I do not exaggerate, unconsciously and unintentionally, the scantiness of my resources and the difficulties of my life. I know that if a shilling or so were given me by anyone, I spent it in a dinner or a tea. I know that I worked, from morning to night, with common men and boys, a shabby child. I know that I tried, but ineffectually, not to anticipate my money, and to make it last the week through, by putting it away in a drawer I had in the countinghouse, wrapped into six little parcels, each parcel containing the same amount and labeled with a different day. I know that I have lounged about the streets, insufficiently and unsatisfactorily fed. I know that, but for the mercy of God, I might easily have been, for any care that was taken of me, a little robber or a little vagabond.

Ask, **How did Charles Dickens spend his money when he was almost as poor as the poor widow?** Have the children consider if spending money on food is acceptable to God. Ask, **Even though Dickens does not tell us that he gave any of his money to persons even less fortunate than he, how do we know that he believed and trusted in God to protect him from his poverty?**

• Prayer •

God, You have given us so much to be thankful for. We are reminded that it is Your plan to give back some of what we have, both to Your church and to others in need. Amen.

═ Lesson Ten ═

⌐ Jesus Calls Children to Him ⌐

• Activity •

Play the telephone game by drawing the name of one child from the Lot Box and asking the child to whisper a message to the child next to him or her. That child then whispers the message to another, and so on, until the last child hears the message and states it aloud, for comparison with the first version, as now revealed by the first child. This activity can even be implemented with very few children. Just be certain that the original message is long, has been written on a sheet of paper, and is initially read from the paper in a whisper, before it is passed on from memory.

Ask, **Does God have messages for us about how He wants us to live our lives? What would have happened if God had given these messages to Jesus, but then no one had ever written down what Jesus said? What do we read in order to learn God's messages to us?**

• The Life of Our Lord •

The disciples asked [Jesus], "Master, who is greatest in the Kingdom of Heaven?" Jesus called a little child to Him, and took him in His arms and stood him among them, and answered, "A child like this. I say unto you that none but those who are as humble as little children shall enter into heaven. Whosoever shall receive one such little child in My name receiveth Me. But whosoever hurts one of them, it were better for him that he had a millstone tied about his neck and were drowned in the depths of the sea. The angels are all children." Our Savior loved the child

and loved all children. Yes, and all the world. No one ever loved all people so well and so truly as He did. [Text: Matthew 18:1-6, 10; Mark 9:33-37; and Luke 9:46-48 and 17:2]

Ask, **Is Jesus saying that heaven is for children only?** It may be necessary to let the children hear the passage again.

Say, **Jesus is teaching about heaven by making a comparison: heaven is for adults, too, but they need to be like children.**

In preparation for Lesson Eleven, ask, **What behavior does Jesus specifically name as making anyone acceptable to God in heaven?** Briefly introduce the term "humble" and the concept of humility.

• Another Thought •

Charles Dickens wrote a book titled *Dombey and Son.* In this book, Mr. Dombey gives most of his love and attention to his son Paul and very little to his daughter Florence. When Paul dies, Mr. Dombey rejects Florence's love and acts as if he has no other children. Mr. Dombey does not even want his second wife, Edith, to love Florence:

One exquisite unhappiness…Florence was spared. She never had the least suspicion that [her stepmother] Edith by her tenderness for her widened the separation from her father, or gave him new cause of dislike. If Florence had conceived the possibility of such an effect being wrought by such a cause, what grief she would have felt, what sacrifice she would have tried to make, poor loving girl, how fast and sure her quiet passage might have been beneath it to the presence of that higher Father who does not reject His children's love, or spurn their tried and broken hearts, Heaven knows! But it was otherwise, and that was well.

Ask, **How do we know that Florence's stepmother loves her? How would Florence know that her stepmother loves her? Why is Florence's father angry with Florence? How should her father treat her? Who does Dickens tell us is the one Father who never rejects His children's love? Who are God's children?**

• Prayer •

God, we are all Your children, no matter how old we are. Thank You for loving us just the way we are. Amen.

Lesson Eleven

⌒ Humility: Part One ⌒

• Activity •

Have the children stand around a table, with an open box of toothpicks in the middle. Draw one child's name from the Lot Box to determine who selects the first toothpick. Tell the children that they are to take turns, one child with one toothpick at a time, making a flat picture of a church on the table, using only toothpicks. Each time a toothpick is added, it must touch a toothpick that is already in place. Allow the children to continue taking turns in a clockwise direction until the picture has been completed. Have them remain standing around the table while the following passage from *The Life of Our Lord* is read aloud.

• The Life of Our Lord •

[Jesus] taught His disciples in stories, because He knew the people liked to hear them and would remember what He said better, if He said it in that way. They are called "parables," the parables of our Savior, and I wish you to remember that word, as I shall soon have some more of these parables to tell you about...

And among other parables, Christ said to these same Pharisees, because of their pride, that two men once went up into the temple to pray, of whom one was a Pharisee and one a publican. The Pharisee said, "God, I thank Thee that I am not unjust as other men are or bad as this publican is!" The publican, standing afar off, would not lift up his eyes to heaven, but struck his breast and only said, "God, be merciful to me, a sinner!" And God, our

Savior told them, would be merciful to that man rather than the other and would be better pleased with his prayer, because he made it with a humble and lowly heart. [Text: Luke 18:9-14]

With the children still standing around their toothpick church, ask, **Who is standing nearest the church's main entrance? If this were a real church, would standing nearest the main entrance make a person better than everyone else? Who is standing farthest from the main entrance? If this were a real church, would standing farthest from the main entrance make a person less acceptable to God? Where would the Pharisee be standing? Why? Where would the publican be standing? Why?** Discuss what it means to have a humble heart.

• Another Thought •

We first met Pip in Lesson Four. Pip is the boy who stole a metal file in *Great Expectations* and then was afraid to tell the truth about his sin. Much later in the book, Pip is a young man, and he is trying to comfort Magwitch, a criminal who is dying. Pip asks him:

"Are you in much pain today?"

"I don't complain of none, dear boy."

"You never do complain."

He had spoken his last words. He smiled, and I understood his touch to mean that he wished to lift my hand, and lay it on his breast. I laid it there, and he smiled again, and put both his hands upon it.

"Dear Magwitch, I must tell you, now at last. You understand what I say?"

A gentle pressure on my hand.

"You had a child once, whom you loved and lost."

55

A stronger pressure on my hand.

"She lived and found powerful friends. She is living now. She is a lady and very beautiful. And I love her!"

With a last faint effort, which would have been powerless but for my yielding to it and assisting it, he raised my hand to his lips. Then he gently let it sink upon his breast again, with his own hands lying on it. The placid look at the white ceiling came back, and passed away, and his head dropped quietly on his breast.

Mindful, then, of what we had read together, I thought of the two men who went up into the temple to pray, and I knew there were no better words that I could say beside his bed than, "O Lord, be merciful to him, a sinner!"

Tell the children that Pip is the "dear boy" to whom Magwitch speaks. Ask, **Is Pip being like the Pharisee when he says of Magwitch, "O Lord, be merciful to him, a sinner?" What would the Pharisee have said about Magwitch? What would the Pharisee have said about himself? What should the Pharisee say about himself?**

• Prayer •

God, You have asked us to be humble in our faith. We promise not to judge others and their relationship with You, but to work harder at being more like Jesus ourselves. Amen.

Lesson Twelve

☞ Humility: Part Two ☜

• Activity •

Use the Lot Box to group the children into pairs. Give each team a poster board or large sheet of paper, a magazine that contains pictures of groups of people, scissors and a glue stick.

Instruct each team to find, cut out and glue on the top half of the poster board three pictures that show one person who seems to be in a place of honor, compared to everyone else in the picture. In addition, have each team find, cut out and glue on the bottom half of the poster board three pictures that show someone who does not seem to be in a place of honor. The selected person in each picture should not be revealed to other teams. Rather, let the teams take turns guessing who is the selected person in each picture.

• The Life of Our Lord •

[Jesus] told them this parable, of which the meaning is that we are never to be proud or think ourselves very good before God, but are always to be humble. He said, "When you are invited to a feast or wedding, do not sit down in the best place, lest some more honored man should come and claim that seat. But sit down in the lowest place, and a better will be offered you if you deserve it. For whosoever exalteth himself shall be abased, and whosoever humbleth himself shall be exalted." [Text: Luke 14:7-11]

Teach that "exalt" means "increase in importance" and "abase" mean "decrease in importance." Reread the last sentence as "whoever increases himself in importance will be decreased in importance, and whoever humbles himself will be increased in importance." Ask, **Which word is similar in meaning to humble: exalt or abase?** Have the children explain how they knew from a picture that someone seemed to be exalted and that someone else seemed to be humble. Discuss why God expects us to be humble before Him.

• Another Thought •

Charles Dickens wrote in *A Christmas Carol*:

[Scrooge] passed the door a dozen times, before he had the courage to go up and knock. But he made a dash and did it:

"Is your master at home, my dear?" said Scrooge to the girl. Nice girl! Very.

"Yes, sir."

"Where is he, my love?" said Scrooge.

"He's in the dining room, sir, along with Mistress. I'll show you upstairs, if you please."

"Thank'ee. He knows me," said Scrooge, with his hand already on the dining room lock. "I'll go in here, my dear."

He turned it gently and sidled his face in, round the door. They were looking at the table (which was spread out in great array), for these young housekeepers are always nervous on such points and like to see that everything is right. "Fred!" said Scrooge.

Dear heart alive, how his niece by marriage started! Scrooge had forgotten, for the moment, about her sitting in the corner with the footstool, or he wouldn't have done it, on any account.

"Why bless my soul!" cried Fred. "Who's that?"

"It's I. Your Uncle Scrooge. I have come to dinner. Will you let me in, Fred?"

Ask, **Is Scrooge claiming a place of honor at Fred's dinner, or is he being humble? How do you know?**

• Prayer •

God, we know we should come before You humbly because You are so great. You have power over our lives, so we will honor You as the King of our lives. Amen.

⌒ Humility: Part Three ⌒

• Activity •

Give each child a pencil and a sheet of drawing paper on which to trace the outline of his or her hand. Then distribute scissors and have the children cut out their drawn hands. Ask each child to think of five different ways he or she could lend a "helping hand" in the service of others. Instruct them to write each way on one of the five fingers. Allow each child to tell the others his or her five ways.

• The Life of Our Lord •

One night, at that place, [Jesus] rose from supper at which He was seated with His disciples, and taking a cloth and a basin of water, washed their feet. Simon Peter, one of the disciples, would have prevented Him from washing his feet, but our Savior told him that He did this in order that they, remembering it, might be always kind and gentle to one another, and might know no pride or ill will among themselves. [Text: John 13:4-17]

Ask, **What makes washing another person's feet an act of humility? What makes lending a "helping hand" to another person an act of humility?**

• Another Thought •

From a letter of advice written by Charles Dickens to his son Henry:

Whatever you do, above all other things, keep out of debt and confide in me. If ever you find yourself on the verge of any perplexity or difficulty, come to me. You will never find me hard with you while you are manly and truthful.

As your brothers have gone away one by one, I have written to each of them what I am now going to write to you. You know that you have never been hampered with religious forms of restraint, and that with mere unmeaning forms I have no sympathy. But I most strongly and affectionately impress upon you the priceless value of the New Testament and the study of that Book as the one unfailing guide in life. Deeply respecting it, and bowing down before the character of our Savior, as separated from the vain constructions and inventions of men, you cannot go very wrong and will always preserve at heart a true spirit of veneration and humility.

Have the children identify the advice which Dickens gave to his son Henry. Ask, **What kind of father does Dickens seem to be to his children? According to Dickens, where should Henry go to learn how to have humility? Where should we go both to learn how to have humility and to learn what kind of Father God is to us?**

• Prayer •

God, You have given us Your Word, the Bible, to show us how to live. Help us to remember to turn to it when we need guidance. We know that we can also talk to You anytime we need You. Amen.

Lesson Fourteen

↢ Miracles: Part One ↣

• Activity •

Place in the Lot Box index cards with one each of the following miracles printed on them:

1. Four men fish all night and catch nothing. They decide to try one last time, and the fish come to them in order to be caught.
2. A man has a skin disease which doctors cannot cure. The disease suddenly goes away.
3. A man's body shakes so much that he cannot walk. Doctors cannot cure him. Suddenly, he walks away, well.
4. A servant is so ill that he cannot make a trip to a doctor's office. The servant's master believes that no doctor needs to visit his servant. The servant becomes well at once.
5. A little girl dies. Someone says that she is only "asleep" and that she will "wake up." She does indeed wake up, alive.
6. A storm is about to sink a boat with men on board. Immediately the storm ends and no one is hurt.
7. A man loses his mind, which causes him to throw himself on sharp stones. Doctors are too afraid to go near him to help him. He sees a herd of pigs and never again throws himself on sharp stones.
8. For thirty-eight years, a man has been too ill to be able to move himself very far. He can be cured only by touching special water, but when he is cured, he has not yet touched the special water.
9. Over five thousand women, children, and men are

hungry. They share and eat five loaves of bread and two fish, and everyone becomes full.

10. Water separates a man from a boat. He walks on top of the water to reach the boat.

Have each child take one of the cards from the Lot Box and give each one time to decide what he or she would need in order to make what the card says come true. (With more than ten children, group the children in pairs and let the partners discuss what they would need.) Let the children share their solutions, or, if they do not have a solution, ask for suggestions from others. After everyone has reported, ask, **Are these solutions difficult or easy to accomplish? Why?**

• The Life of Our Lord •

When [Jesus] came out of the Wilderness, He began to cure sick people by only laying His hand upon them, for God had given Him power to heal the sick, and to give sight to the blind, and to do many wonderful and solemn things of which I shall tell you more by and by and which are called the miracles of Christ. I wish you would remember that word, because I shall use it again, and I should like you to know that it means something which is very wonderful and which could not be done without God's leave and assistance.

The first miracle which Jesus Christ did was at a place called Cana, where He went to a marriage feast with Mary, His mother. There was no wine, and Mary told Him so. There were only six stone water pots filled with water. But Jesus turned this water into wine by only lifting up His hand, and all who were there drank of it.

For God had given Jesus Christ the power to do such wonders, and He did them that people might know He was not a common man and might believe what He taught them, and also believe that God had sent Him. And many people, hearing this and hearing that He cured the sick, did begin to believe in Him, and great crowds followed Him in the streets and on the roads, wherever He went. [Text: Matthew 4:24-25; Luke 4:14; and John 2:1-11]

Ask, **Who is responsible for all miracles? How would Jesus have felt before and after curing a sick person? Why? How would the sick person feel before and after the cure? Why?**

• Another Thought •

Charles Dickens wrote in *A Christmas Carol:*

"There's father coming," cried the two young Cratchits, who were everywhere at once. "Hide, Martha, hide!"

So Martha hid herself, and in came little Bob, the father, with at least three feet of comforter exclusive of the fringe, hanging down before him; and his threadbare clothes darned up and brushed, to look seasonable; and Tiny Tim upon his shoulder. Alas for Tiny Tim, he bore a little crutch, and had his limbs supported by an iron frame!

"Why, where's our Martha?" cried Bob Cratchit, looking round.

"Not coming," said Mrs. Cratchit.

"Not coming!" said Bob, with a sudden declension in his high spirits, for he had been Tim's blood horse all the way from church and had come home rampant. "Not coming upon Christmas Day!"

Martha didn't like to see him disappointed, if it were only in joke, so she came out prematurely from behind

the closet door and ran into his arms, while the two young Cratchits hustled Tiny Tim and bore him off into the washhouse, that he might hear the pudding singing in the copper.

"And how did little Tim behave?" asked Mrs. Cratchit, when she had rallied Bob on his credulity, and Bob had hugged his daughter to his heart's content.

"As good as gold," said Bob, "and better. Somehow he gets thoughtful, sitting by himself so much, and thinks the strangest things you ever heard. He told me, coming home, that he hoped the people saw him in the church, because he was a cripple, and it might be pleasant to them to remember upon Christmas Day, who made lame beggars walk and blind men see."

Ask, **Is it possible for you to help others without an actual miracle happening?** Review with them their promises displayed from Lesson Eight and their suggestions for helping others from Lesson Nine.

• Prayer •

We know that You are the Creator of miracles, God, and that sometimes miracles still occur. But we also know that You give us the ability to help people every day. Show us the ways You would have us help others so we can be more like You. Amen.

☞ Miracles: Part Two ☜

• Activity •

Read aloud the first miracle from its index card created for Lesson Fourteen. If any of the children have ever read or heard about this miracle in the Bible, ask them to tell what they remember. Then read aloud the corresponding excerpt below from *The Life of Our Lord.*

Next, read aloud the second miracle from its index card created for Lesson Fourteen. Again, if any of the children are familiar with this miracle, ask them to tell what they remember before reading aloud the corresponding excerpt below. Follow the same steps for the third, fourth and fifth miracles.

• The Life of Our Lord •

1. The first four of these were poor fishermen, who were sitting in their boats by the seaside, mending their nets, when Christ passed by. He stopped and went into Simon Peter's boat and asked him if he had caught many fish. Peter said no; though they had worked all night with their nets, they had caught nothing. Christ said, "Let down the net again." They did so, and it was immediately so full of fish that it required the strength of many men (who came and helped them) to lift it out of the water, and even then it was very hard to do. This was another of the miracles of Jesus Christ. [Text: Matthew 4:18-22; Mark 1:16-20; and Luke 5:1-11]

2. When [Jesus] was come down from the mountain, there came to Him a man with a dreadful disease

called the leprosy. It was common in those times, and those who were ill with it were called lepers. This leper fell at the feet of Jesus Christ and said, "Lord! If Thou wilt, Thou canst make me well!" Jesus, always full of compassion, stretched out His hand and said, "I will! Be thou well!" And his disease went away, immediately, and he was cured. [Text: Matthew 8:1-3; Mark 1:40-42; and Luke 5:12-13]

3. Being followed wherever He went by great crowds of people, Jesus went with His disciples into a house to rest. While He was sitting inside, some men brought upon a bed a man who was very ill of what is called the palsy, so that he trembled all over from head to foot and could neither stand nor move. But the crowd being all about the door and windows, and they not being able to get near Jesus Christ, these men climbed up to the roof of the house, which was a low one, and through the tiling at the top let down the bed with the sick man upon it, into the room where Jesus sat. When He saw him, Jesus, full of pity, said, "Arise! Take up thy bed, and go to thine own home!" And the man rose up and went away quite well, blessing Him and thanking God. [Text: Matthew 9:1-8; Mark 2:1-12; Luke 5:15, 17-20 and 24-25]

4. There was a centurion, too, or officer over the soldiers, who came to Him and said, "Lord! My servant lies at home in my house, very ill." Jesus Christ made answer, "I will come and cure him." But the centurion said, "Lord! I am not worthy that Thou shouldst come to my house. Say the word only, and I know he will be cured." Then Jesus Christ, glad that the centurion believed in Him so truly, said, "Be it so!" And the servant became well, from that moment. [Text: Matthew 8:5-13; Luke 7:1-10]

5. But of all the people who came to [Jesus], none was so full of grief and distress as one man who was a ruler or magistrate over many people, and he wrung his hands and cried and said, "Oh, Lord, my daughter, my beautiful, good, innocent, little girl is dead. Oh, come to her, come to her, and lay Thy blessed hand upon her, and I know she will revive and come to life again and make me and her mother happy. Oh, Lord, we love her so, we love her so! And she is dead!" Jesus Christ went out with him, and so did His disciples, and went to his house, where the friends and neighbors were crying in the room where the poor dead little girl lay and where there was soft music playing, as there used to be in those days when people died. Jesus Christ, looking on her sorrowfully, said to comfort her poor parents, "She is not dead. She is asleep." Then He commanded the room to be cleared of the people who were in it, and going to the dead child, took her by the hand, and she rose up, quite well, as if she had only been asleep. Oh, what a sight it must have been to see her parents clasp her in their arms and kiss her and thank God and Jesus Christ, His Son, for such great mercy! [Text: Matthew 9:18-19, 23-25; Mark 5:22-24, 35-43; and Luke 8:41-42, 49-56]

Review with the children God's essential role in any miracle. Then discuss the ability we have to help others by means other than miracles.

• Another Thought •

We first met the seven poor travelers in Lesson Five, when they shared a meal together on Christmas Eve. Now

it is Christmas Day:

In time, the distant river with the ships came full in view, and with it pictures of the poor fishermen, mending their nets, who arose and followed Him, — of the teaching of the people from a ship pushed off a little way from shore, by reason of the multitude, — of a majestic figure walking on the water, in the loneliness of night. My very shadow on the ground was eloquent of Christmas, for did not the people lay their sick where the mere shadows of the men who had heard and seen Him might fall as they passed along?

For Charles Dickens, a river, ships and even shadows reminded him of Jesus. Discuss with the children what in our lives today can remind us of Jesus. Ask, **How can thinking about Jesus help us be better persons and make better decisions about how we treat each other in today's world?**

• Prayer •

God, we see You all around us every day, in Your creation, in our Christian friends and family, and in the Bible. Remind us, God, to always treat others as You would treat them, whether it be to help, to comfort or just to love. Amen.

❧ Miracles: Part Three ❧

• Activity •

Read aloud the sixth miracle from its index card created for Lesson Fourteen. If any of the children have ever read or heard about this miracle in the Bible, ask them to tell what they remember. Then read aloud the corresponding excerpt below from *The Life of Our Lord.*

Next, read aloud the seventh miracle from its index card created for Lesson Fourteen. Again, if any of the children are familiar with this miracle, ask them to tell what they remember before reading aloud the corresponding excerpt. Follow the same steps for the eighth, ninth and tenth miracles.

• The Life of Our Lord •

6. By this time the crowd was so very great that Jesus Christ went down to the waterside, to go in a boat to a more retired place. And in the boat He fell asleep, while His disciples were sitting on the deck. While He was still sleeping, a violent storm arose, so that the waves washed over the boat, and the howling wind so rocked and shook it, that they thought it would sink. In their fright the disciples awoke our Savior and said, "Lord! Save us, or we are lost!" He stood up and, raising His arm, said to the rolling sea and to the whistling wind, "Peace! Be still!" And immediately it was calm and pleasant weather, and the boat went safely on through the smooth waters. [Text: Matthew 8:23-26; Mark

4:35-41; and Luke 8:22-25]

7. When they came to the other side of the waters, they had to pass a wild and lonely burying ground that was outside the city to which they were going. All burying grounds were outside cities in those times. In this place there was a dreadful madman who lived among the tombs and howled all day and night, so that it made travelers afraid, to hear him. They had tried to chain him, but he broke his chains—he was so strong—and he would throw himself on the sharp stones and cut himself in the most dreadful manner, crying and howling all the while. When this wretched man saw Jesus Christ a long way off, he cried out, "It is the Son of God! Oh, Son of God, do not torment me!" Jesus, coming near him, perceived that he was torn by an evil spirit and cast the madness out of him and into a herd of swine (or pigs) which were feeding close by and which directly ran headlong down a steep place leading to the sea and were dashed to pieces. [Text: Matthew 8:28-34; Mark 5:1-13; and Luke 8:26-33]

8. There was, near the sheep market in that place, a pool or pond, called Bethesda, having five gates to it, and at the time of the year when that feast took place great numbers of sick people and cripples went to this pool to bathe in it, believing that an angel came and stirred the water, and that whoever went in first after the angel had done so was cured of any illness he or she had, whatever it might be. Among these poor persons was one man who had been ill thirty-eight years, and he told Jesus Christ (who took pity on him when He saw him lying on his bed alone, with no one to help him) that he never could be dipped in the pool, because he was so weak and ill that he could not move to get there. Our Savior said to him, "Take up

thy bed and go away." And he went away, quite well. [Text: John 5:1-9]

9. Jesus, going with His disciples over a sea called the Sea of Tiberias and sitting with them on a hillside, saw great numbers of these poor people waiting below and said to the apostle Philip, "Where shall we buy bread, that they may eat and be refreshed after their long journey?" Philip answered, "Lord, two hundred pennyworth of bread would not be enough for so many people, and we have none." "We have only," said another apostle—Andrew, Simon Peter's brother—"five small barley loaves and two little fish, belonging to a lad who is among us. What are they, among so many!" Jesus Christ said, "Let them all sit down!" They did, there being a great deal of grass in that place. When they were all seated, Jesus took the bread and looked up to Heaven and blessed it, and broke it, and handed it in pieces to the apostles, who handed it to the people. And of those five little loaves and two fish, five thousand men, besides women and children, ate and had enough, and when they were all satisfied, there were gathered up twelve baskets full of what was left. This was another of the miracles of Jesus Christ. [Text: Matthew 14:14-21; Mark 6:32-44; Luke 9:10-17; and John 6:1-14]

10. Our Savior then sent His disciples away in a boat across the water and said He would follow them presently, when He had dismissed the people. The people being gone, He remained by Himself to pray, so that the night came on, and the disciples were still rowing on the water in their boat, wondering when Christ would come. Late in the night, when the wind was against them and the waves

were running high, they saw Him coming walking towards them on the water, as if it were dry land. When they saw this, they were terrified and cried out, but Jesus said, "It is I. Be not afraid!" Peter, taking courage, said, "Lord, if it be Thou, tell me to come to Thee upon the water." Jesus Christ said, "Come!" Peter then walked towards Him, but seeing the angry waves and hearing the wind roar, he was frightened and began to sink, and would have done so but that Jesus took him by the hand and led him into the boat. Then, in a moment, the wind went down, and the disciples said to one another, "It is true! He is the Son of God!" [Text: Matthew 14:22-33; Mark 6:45-52; and John 6:16-21]

Ask, **Should we ever pray to God for a miracle? Should we ask God to help someone else in whatever way He knows is best, or should we tell God what He needs to do? If we can help someone in need, should we ask God to do it for us? Why not?**

• Another Thought •

Charles Dickens gave a speech about schools, where he said:

And now, ladies and gentlemen, perhaps you will permit me to sketch in a few words the sort of school that I do like…. [I]t is a place of education where…the beautiful history of the Christian religion is daily taught and…the life of that Divine Teacher who Himself took little children on His knees is daily studied.

Ask, **What do Jesus' miracles teach us about Jesus? What do Jesus' miracles teach us about God? Did Dickens believe that we should learn about Jesus only** in church? **How do we know?**

• Prayer •

God, we know that You are in control of everything. Sometimes, though, we think we need to control a situation. Help us to remember that You are in charge, and that You want us to learn about You throughout our lives, not just at church. Our lives are Yours, God. Amen.

⌒ Good Deeds ⌒

• Activity •

A calendar that provides room for recording information below each date is needed for this activity. If there are less than twelve children, tear off a month for each child. If there are more than twelve, assign partners to each month.

Give the children pencils and ask them to think of seven good deeds that anyone could perform. Each time they decide on a good deed, they are to choose a date on their month under which to record it. For example, one month might have good deeds on the 18th, 19th, 20th, 21st, 22nd, 23rd and 24th, while another month might have them recorded on the 1st, 2nd, 7th, 12th, 13th, 18th and 28th.

Display the months and have the children explain their seven good deeds to everyone else. On a poster board or a large sheet of paper, make a number tally of how many times each day of the week was selected by the children.

• The Life of Our Lord •

There were in that country where our Savior performed His miracles certain people who were called Pharisees. They were very proud and believed that no people were good but themselves, and they were all afraid of Jesus Christ, because He taught the people better. So were the Jews, in general. Most of the inhabitants of that country were Jews.

Our Savior, walking once in the fields with His disciples on a Sunday—which the Jews called and still call

the Sabbath—they gathered some ears of the corn that were growing there, to eat. This, the Pharisees said, was wrong, and in the same way, when our Savior went into one of their churches—they were called synagogues—and looked compassionately on a poor man who had his hand all withered and wasted away, these Pharisees said, "Is it right to cure people on a Sunday?" Our Savior answered them by saying, "If any of you had a sheep and it fell into a pit, would you not take it out, even though it happened on a Sunday? And how much better is a man than a sheep!" Then He said to the poor man, "Stretch out thine hand!" And it was cured immediately and was smooth and useful like the other. So Jesus Christ told them, "You may always do good, no matter what the day is." [Text: Matthew 12:1-2, 9-13; Mark 2:23-24; 3:1-6; and Luke 6:1-2, 6-11]

If there are any marks on the board for Sunday, ask those who placed them there to read those deeds aloud. Ask, **Would Jesus approve of doing those deeds on Sunday?** If there are no marks on the board for Sunday, ask, **Would Jesus approve of the good deeds you have listed being done on a Sunday?**

• Another Thought •

Charles Dickens wrote to Baroness Burdett-Coutts:

I don't know whether you have seen an advertisement in the papers of this morning, signed by me, and having reference to the family of Mr. Elton, that actor who was drowned in the Pegasus. I consented last night to act as chairman of a committee for the assistance of his children: and I assure you that their condition is melancholy and desolate beyond all painting.

He was a struggling man through his whole existence—always very poor and never extravagant. His wife died mad, three years ago, and he was left a widower with seven children—who were expecting his knock at the door, when a friend arrived with the terrible news of his death.

Ask, **What days of the week would orphans need food, clothing and shelter? Would Jesus turn these children away on any day? How did Dickens try to help them?**

• Prayer •

You have shown us that we should live for You every day, God, not simply on Sunday. We will try to do something good for You each day. Amen.

Lesson Eighteen

❧ Forgiveness: Part One ❧

• Activity •

Distribute construction paper, markers and rulers to the children. Direct each child to divide his or her paper into two equal portions with a straight line. On one half, instruct the children to draw a picture of how they feel after accidentally doing wrong to someone else. On the other half, have them draw a picture of how they feel when the wronged person does not get angry or upset.

When the pictures have been completed, but before they have been put on display, ask, **Even though everyone drew a different picture about how it feels to do something wrong accidentally, what should be the same in all of these pictures?**

Continue, **Even though everyone drew a different picture about how it feels when the wronged person does not get angry or upset, what should be the same in all of the pictures? Why do we feel better when the wronged person does not get angry or upset?** Put the pictures on display, and see if they are similar in the ways expected.

• The Life of Our Lord •

As great crowds of people followed [Jesus] and wished to be taught, He went up into a mountain and there preached to them and gave them, from His own lips, the words of that prayer beginning, "Our Father which art in Heaven," that you say every night. It is called the Lord's Prayer, because it was first said by Jesus Christ and because He commanded His disciples to pray in those words....

One of the Pharisees begged our Savior to go into his house and eat with him. And while our Savior sat eating at the table, there crept into the room a woman of that city who had led a bad and sinful life, and was ashamed that the Son of God should see her; and yet she trusted so much to His goodness and His compassion for all who, having done wrong, were truly sorry for it in their hearts, that, by little and little, she went behind the seat on which He sat, and dropped down at His feet, and wetted them with her sorrowful tears. Then she kissed them and dried them on her long hair, and rubbed them with some sweet smelling ointment she had brought with her in a box. Her name was Mary, and she was from Bethany.

When the Pharisee saw that Jesus permitted this woman to touch Him, he said within himself that Jesus did not know how wicked she had been. But Jesus Christ, who knew his thoughts, said to him, "Simon"—for that was his name—"if a man had debtors, one of whom owed him five hundred pence, and one of whom owed him only fifty pence, and he forgave them both their debts, which of those two debtors do you think would love him most?" Simon answered, "I suppose that one whom he forgave most." Jesus told him he was right and said, "As God forgives this woman so much sin, she will love Him, I hope, the more." And He said to her, "God forgives you!" The company who were present wondered that Jesus Christ had power to forgive sins, but God had given it to Him. And the woman, thanking Him for all His mercy, went away.

We learn from this that we must always forgive those who have done us any harm, when they come to us and say they are truly sorry for it. Even if they do not come and say so, we must still forgive them and never hate them or be unkind to them, if we would hope that God will forgive us....

Peter asked Him, "Lord, how often shall I forgive anyone who offends me? Seven times?" Our Savior answered, "Seventy times seven times, and more than that. For how can you hope that God will forgive you, when you do wrong, unless you forgive all other people!"

And He told His disciples this story. He said, "There was once a servant who owed his master a great deal of money and could not pay it, at which the master, being very angry, was going to have this servant sold for a slave. But the servant, kneeling down and begging his master's pardon with great sorrow, the master forgave him. Now this same servant had a fellow servant who owed him a hundred pence, and instead of being kind and forgiving to this poor man, as his master had been to him, he put him in prison for the debt. His master, hearing of it, went to him and said, 'Oh, wicked servant, I forgave you. Why did you not forgive your fellow servant!' And because he had not done so, his master turned him away with great misery."

"So," said our Savior, "how can you expect God to forgive you, if you do not forgive others!" This is the meaning of that part of the Lord's Prayer where we say, "Forgive us our trespasses"—that word means faults—"as we forgive them that trespass against us." [Text: Matthew 5:1-2, 6:9-13 and 18:21-35; Luke 7:36-50 and 11:2-4]

Ask for a volunteer to recite the Lord's Prayer, and then discuss the meaning of each part of the prayer. Ask, **When someone forgives us for doing something wrong, should that person remain angry or upset with us? When Jesus forgives our sins, how should we feel?**

• Another Thought •

Charles Dickens wrote a book titled *Bleak House*.
This book tells about a boy named Jo, who is as poor
as we learned Oliver was in Lesson Two. When Jo is
dying, his friend Mr. Woodcourt asks:

"Jo, can you say what I say?"

"I'll say anythink as you say, sir, fur I knows it's good."

"OUR FATHER."

"Our Father! —yes, that's wery good, sir."

"WHICH ART IN HEAVEN."

"Art in Heaven—is the light a-comin, sir?"

"It is close at hand. HALLOWED BE THY NAME!"

"Hallowed be—thy—"

Say, **Jo does not continue, because he has died.
Why would Mr. Woodcourt think it is so important
for Jo to pray to God before he dies? Why did he select
the Lord's Prayer for Jo to repeat? Why would Charles
Dickens want to make us think about the Lord's
Prayer when we read one of his books?**

• Prayer •

Thank You, God, for showing us how to pray with
the Lord's Prayer. There is so much for us to learn about
prayer in those words. Guide us as we try to live out what
that prayer says. Amen.

⤳ Compassion ⤝

• Activity •

Use the Lot Box to assign the children to groups of three. Give each group a clothes hanger, scissors, string, drawing paper and colored pencils. Instruct the groups to make a mobile consisting of one man and two women by drawing and cutting out figures. On one side of the man and each woman, the faces should be sad. On the other side, the faces should be happy. Let the children use a hole punch after they complete their pictures to attach the pictures to the hanger by threading string through them. Display the finished mobiles.

• The Life of Our Lord •

There was a certain man named Lazarus of Bethany, who was taken very ill, and as he was the brother of that Mary who had anointed Christ with ointment and wiped His feet with her hair, she and her sister Martha sent to Him in great trouble, saying, "Lord, Lazarus whom You love is sick and likely to die."

Jesus did not go to them for two days after receiving this message, but when that time was past, He said to His disciples, "Lazarus is dead. Let us go to Bethany." When they arrived there—it was a place very near to Jerusalem— they found, as Jesus had foretold, that Lazarus was dead and had been dead and buried four days.

When Martha heard that Jesus was coming, she rose up from among the people who had come to condole with her on her poor brother's death and ran to meet Him, leaving her sister Mary weeping in the house. When

Martha saw Him, she burst into tears and said, "Oh, Lord, if Thou hadst been here, my brother would not have died." "Thy brother shall rise again," returned our Savior. "I know he will, and I believe he will, Lord, at the resurrection on the last day," said Martha.

Jesus said to her, "I am the resurrection and the life. Dost thou believe this?" She answered, "Yes, Lord," and running back to her sister Mary, told her that Christ had come. Mary, hearing this, ran out, followed by all those who had been grieving with her in the house, and coming to the place where He was, fell down at His feet upon the ground and wept, and so did all the rest. Jesus was so full of compassion for their sorrow that He wept, too, as He said, "Where have you laid him?" They said, "Lord, come and see!"

He was buried in a cave, and there was a great stone laid upon it. When they all came to the grave, Jesus ordered the stone to be rolled away, which was done. Then, after casting up His eyes and thanking God, He said in a loud and solemn voice, "Lazarus, come forth!" And the dead man, Lazarus, restored to life, came out among the people and went home with his sisters. At this sight, so awful and affecting, many of the people there believed that Christ was indeed the Son of God, come to instruct and save mankind. But others ran to tell the Pharisees, and from that day the Pharisees resolved among themselves—to prevent more people from believing in Him—that Jesus should be killed. And they agreed among themselves, meeting in the Temple for that purpose, that if He came into Jerusalem before the Feast of the Passover, which was then approaching, He should be seized. [Text: John 11:1-7, 14, 17-47, 53, and 55-57]

Ask, **Do both sides of the pictures of women on your mobiles show the feelings of Mary and Martha? Why?**

Do the pictures of men show the feelings of Jesus? **How do you know?** Discuss the meaning of the word "compassion," which Jesus felt for Mary and Martha. Then ask, **What would two sides of a picture of Lazarus need to look like?**

• Another Thought •

Charles Dickens wrote many short stories. We have already heard twice about *The Seven Poor Travelers.* In *The Wreck of the Golden Mary,* twenty travelers are sailing from England to America, but three-year-old Lucy becomes ill and dies in her mother's arms:

All that thirteenth night, Miss Coleshaw, lying across my knees as I kept the helm, comforted and supported the poor mother. Her child, covered with a pea jacket of mine, lay in her lap. It troubled me all night to think that there was no prayer book among us, and that I could remember but very few of the exact words of the burial service.

When I stood up at broad day, all knew what was going to be done, and I noticed that my poor fellows made the motion of uncovering their heads, though their heads had been stark bare to the sky and sea for many a weary hour. There was a long heavy swell on, but otherwise it was a fair morning, and there were broad fields of sunlight on the waves in the east. I said no more than this: "'I am the resurrection and the life', saith the Lord. He raised the daughter of Jairus the ruler, and said she was not dead but slept. He raised the widow's son. He arose Himself and was seen of many. He loved little children, saying, 'Suffer them to come unto me, and rebuke them not, for of such is the kingdom of Heaven.' In His name, my friends, and committed to His merciful goodness!" With those words

I laid my rough face softly on the placid little forehead, and buried [the child].

Ask, **Did Jesus raise back to life anyone besides Lazarus? Whom did He raise? Who raised Jesus after He was put to death? Who will raise to eternal life with God those of us who accept Jesus as our Lord and Savior? How do we know that God has compassion for us?**

• Prayer •

Jesus, we are so happy that You promise to take us to heaven with You if we accept You as our Lord and Savior. Thank You for having compassion for us. Help us to show Your compassion to others. Amen.

Lesson Twenty

☞ Forgiveness: Part Two ☜

• Activity •

Give each child one paper towel, a paper cup partially filled with water and a fine-tip marker. Have the children carefully draw three separate circles on the paper towel. Next, instruct each child to dip a finger into his or her cup of water and shake off one drop of water into each circle. When the three drops of water have been properly placed, have the children draw three smaller circles, just around the circumference of each drop, again taking care not to tear the paper. Set the paper towels aside to dry. While waiting for the towels to dry, review the following two paragraphs from Lesson Eighteen about Mary of Bethany, and then continue with Dickens' new information about Mary.

• The Life of Our Lord •

One of the Pharisees begged our Savior to go into his house and eat with him. And while our Savior sat eating at the table, there crept into the room a woman of that city who had led a bad and sinful life, and was ashamed that the Son of God should see her; and yet she trusted so much to His goodness and His compassion for all who, having done wrong, were truly sorry for it in their hearts, that, by little and little, she went behind the seat on which He sat, and dropped down at His feet, and wetted them with her sorrowful tears. Then she kissed them and dried them on her long hair, and rubbed them with some sweet smelling ointment she had brought with her in a box. Her name was Mary, and she was from Bethany.

When the Pharisee saw that Jesus permitted this woman to touch Him, he said within himself that Jesus did not know how wicked she had been. But Jesus Christ, who knew his thoughts, said to him, "Simon"—for that was his name—"if a man had debtors, one of whom owed him five hundred pence, and one of whom owed him only fifty pence, and he forgave them both their debts, which of those two debtors do you think would love him most?" Simon answered, "I suppose that one whom he forgave most." Jesus told him he was right and said, "As God forgives this woman so much sin, she will love Him, I hope, the more." And He said to her, "God forgives you!" The company who were present wondered that Jesus Christ had power to forgive sins, but God had given it to Him. And the woman, thanking Him for all His mercy, went away.

It was six days before the Passover, when Jesus raised Lazarus from the dead, and, at night, when they all sat at supper together, with Lazarus among them, Mary rose up and took a pound of ointment—which was very precious and costly, and was called ointment of spikenard—and anointed the feet of Jesus Christ with it, and, once again, wiped them on her hair, and the whole house was filled with the pleasant smell of the ointment. Judas Iscariot, one of the disciples, pretended to be angry at this and said that the ointment might have been sold for three hundred pence, and the money given to the poor. But he only said so, in reality, because he carried the purse and was— unknown to the rest at that time—a thief, and wished to get all the money he could. He now began to plot for betraying Christ into the hands of the chief priests. [Text: Matthew 26:6-9, 14-16; Mark 14:3-6, 10-11; Luke 7:36-50; and John 12:1-6]

Ask, **Who was upset with Mary the first time she**

anointed Jesus' feet? Why? Who was upset with Mary the second time? Why? Was Jesus ever upset with her? How do we know?

Have the children examine their paper towels. Ask, **If each drop of water were a sin, what has happened or is happening to those sins? Who can make real sins disappear? What must we do for this to happen?**

• Another Thought •

In *A Christmas Carol*, Scrooge was shown the future by the Ghost of Christmas Yet to Come. In another of Charles Dickens' Christmas books, *The Chimes*, Toby Veck is shown the future by goblins. In this future, an orphan named Lillian is dying. Before she dies, she wants Toby's daughter Meg, who has been like a mother to Lillian, to forgive her for not being the good person Meg tried to help her to be. Lillian says:

"Forgive me, Meg! So dear, so dear! Forgive me! I know you do, I see you do, but say so, Meg!"

She said so, with her lips on Lillian's cheek. And with her arms twined round—she knew it now—a broken heart.

"[Jesus'] blessing on you, dearest love. Kiss me once more! He suffered her to sit beside His feet and dry them with her hair. O Meg, what mercy and compassion!"

[And] she died....

Ask, **What did Lillian most want from Meg before she died? Why did Lillian ask for Jesus to bless Meg? How did Jesus bless Mary of Bethany?**

• Prayer •

God, You forgive all of our sins and love us equally. Help us to show love and acceptance to others so that we might share with them about Your forgiveness. Amen.

Lesson Twenty-One

⌐ Returning to God ⌐

• Activity •

Use the Lot Box to match each child with one partner. Give each pair five index cards and some markers for writing, one per card, five different things someone who does not care about being a good person might do. Have each pair exchange all five cards for another pair's five cards. Then instruct the children to take turns reading a card aloud and predicting how the person who does not care about being good would behave in each instance if he or she now wanted to please God. Discuss why the new behaviors are so different from the old ones.

• The Life of Our Lord •

It happened that our Savior, being in the city of Jericho, saw, looking down upon Him over the heads of the crowd from a tree into which he had climbed for that purpose, a man named Zacchaeus, who was regarded as a common kind of man and a sinner, but to whom Jesus Christ called out as He passed along that He would come and eat with him in his house that day. Those proud men, the Pharisees and scribes, hearing this, muttered among themselves and said, "He eats with sinners." In answer to them, Jesus related this parable, which is usually called "The Parable of the Prodigal Son."

"There was once a man," He told them, "who had two sons. And the younger of them said one day, 'Father, give me my share of your riches now, and let me do with it what I please.' The father granting his request, he traveled away with his money into a distant country and soon spent it in

riotous living.

"When he had spent all, there came a time, through all that country, of great public distress and famine, when there was no bread, and when the corn and the grass and all the things that grow in the ground were all dried up and blighted. The prodigal son fell into such distress and hunger that he hired himself out as a servant to feed swine in the fields. And he would have been glad to eat even the poor coarse husks that the swine were fed, but his master gave him none. In this distress, he said to himself, 'How many of my father's servants have bread enough and to spare, while I perish with hunger! I will arise and go to my father and will say unto him, "Father! I have sinned against heaven and before thee, and am no more worthy to be called thy son!"'"

"And so he traveled back again, in great pain and sorrow and difficulty, to his father's house. When he was yet a great way off, his father saw him and knew him in the midst of all his rags and misery, and ran towards him, and wept, and fell upon his neck, and kissed him. And he told his servants to clothe this poor repentant son in the best robes and to make a great feast to celebrate his return, which was done, and they began to be merry.

"But the eldest son, who had been in the field and knew nothing of his brother's return, coming to the house and hearing the music and dancing, called to one of the servants and asked him what it meant. To this the servant made answer that his brother had come home and that his father was joyful because of his return. At this, the elder brother was angry and would not go into the house, so the father, hearing of it, came out to persuade him.

"'Father,' said the elder brother, 'you do not treat me justly, to show so much joy for my younger brother's return. For these many years I have remained with you constantly and have been true to you, yet you have never made a feast for me. But when my younger brother returns, who has been prodigal and riotous, and spent his money in many bad ways, you are full of delight, and the whole house makes merry!' 'Son,' returned the father, 'you have always been with me, and all I have is yours. But we thought your brother dead, and he is alive. He was lost, and he is found, and it is natural and right that we should be merry for his unexpected return to his old home.'"

By this, our Savior meant to teach that those who have done wrong and forgotten God are always welcome to Him and will always receive His mercy, if they will only return to Him in sorrow for the sin of which they have been guilty. [Text: Luke 15:11-32; 19:1-7]

Discuss the meaning of the word "prodigal." In the last paragraph of this excerpt from *The Life of Our Lord*, Charles Dickens summarizes Jesus' lesson as it pertains to the prodigal son. Discuss this lesson, and then have the children consider what lesson Jesus also wants us to learn concerning the elder son.

• Another Thought •

Another of Charles Dickens' books is *The Battle of Life*. In this book, thirty-year-old Michael Warden has spent all of his money, borrowed and spent other people's money and now seeks advice from his lawyer, Mr. Snitchey, about whether he can pay anyone back what he owes:

"That's all," said Mr. Snitchey, turning up the last paper. "Really there's no other resource. No other resource."

"All lost, spent, wasted, pawned, borrowed, and sold, eh?" said [Michael Warden], looking up.

"All," returned Mr. Snitchey.

"Nothing else to be done, you say?"

"Nothing at all."

The client bit his nails, and pondered again.

"And I am not even personally safe in England? You hold to that, do you?"

"In no part of the United Kingdom of Great Britain and Ireland," replied Mr. Snitchey.

"A mere prodigal son with no father to go back to, no swine to keep, and no husks to share with them? Eh?" pursued the client, rocking one leg over the other and searching the ground with his eyes.

Ask, **Could someone be a prodigal son or daughter with no parent to return to or with a parent who won't accept the son or daughter?** Emphasize again that we can always return to God when we have done wrong.

• Prayer •

You are always willing to take us back, God, even when we think we have gone away from You forever. Thank You for continuing to love us. Amen.

Lesson Twenty-Two

⮞ Use of Money ⮜

• Activity •

Ask the children to name from memory whose face appears on a penny, a nickel, a dime and a quarter. Have them tell what they know about each president. Then ask them to consider why those presidents are on coins instead of other presidents. Give each child a penny, nickel, dime and quarter. Distribute drawing paper and pencils, and show the children how to reproduce the image of a coin by placing the coin under the paper and lightly shading the part of the paper which is directly over the face of the coin. Have each child do the same with each coin. Then have them cut out the copies. Do not collect the real coins yet.

• The Life of Our Lord •

The Pharisees were so angry at being taught these things that they employed some spies to ask our Savior questions and to try to entrap Him into saying something which was against the law. The emperor of that country, who was called Caesar, commanded tribute money to be regularly paid to him by the people and was cruel against anyone who disputed his right to it. The spies thought they might, perhaps, induce our Savior to say it was an unjust payment and so to bring Himself under the emperor's displeasure. Therefore, pretending to be very humble, they came to Him and said, "Master, You teach the word of God rightly and do not respect persons on account of their wealth or high station. Tell us, is it lawful that we should pay tribute to Caesar?"

Christ, who knew their thoughts, replied, "Why do you ask? Show me a penny." They did so. "Whose image and whose name is this upon it?" He asked them. They said, "Caesar's." "Then," said He, "render unto Caesar the things that are Caesar's." [Text: Matthew 22:15-22; Mark 12:13-17; and Luke 20:20-26]

Review with the children from Lessons Eleven, Twelve and Thirteen the concept of humility. Ask, **Why would the Pharisees pretend to be humble before Jesus?** Discuss what Jesus meant when He said to give to Caesar what already belongs to Caesar, including his coins. Then ask, **Do coins belong to presidents? To whom do they belong? Can God use our coins if we give them to our church? How can God use them?** Collect the coins used in the activity for a church donation.

• Another Thought •

We have already met two characters from *Bleak House* in Lesson Eighteen, Mr. Woodcourt and Jo, the dying boy with whom he began reciting the Lord's Prayer. *Bleak House* also tells of the Pardiggle family, Mrs. Pardiggle and her five sons:

[Mr. Jarndyce] remarked that there were two classes of charitable people: one, the people who did a little and made a great deal of noise; the other, the people who did a great deal and made no noise at all. We were therefore curious to see Mrs. Pardiggle, suspecting her to be a type of the former class, and were glad when she called one day with her five young sons.

She was a formidable style of lady, with spectacles, a prominent nose and a loud voice, who had the effect of wanting a great deal of room. And she really did, for she knocked down little chairs that were a great way off with her skirts. As only Ada and I were at home, we received her timidly, for she seemed to come in like cold weather and to make the little Pardiggles blue as they followed.

"These, young ladies," said Mrs. Pardiggle, with great volubility, after the first salutations, "are my five boys. You may have seen their names in a printed subscription list—perhaps more than one—in the possession of our esteemed friend, Mr. Jarndyce. Egbert, my eldest—twelve—is the boy who sent out his pocket money, to the amount of five and three pence, to the Tockahoopo Indians. Oswald, my second—ten-and-a-half—is the child who contributed two and nine pence to the Great National Smithers Testimonial. Francis, my third—nine—one and six pence halfpenny; Felix, my fourth—seven—eight pence to the Superannuated Widows; Alfred, my youngest—five—has voluntarily enrolled himself in the Infant Bonds of Joy, and is pledged never, through life, to use tobacco in any form."

We had never seen such dissatisfied children. It was not merely that they were wizened and shriveled, though they were certainly that too, but they looked absolutely ferocious with discontent.

Say, **Four of the Pardiggle boys are donating their coins to charity. Why are they dissatisfied and discontented? Who seems to be telling them when to donate, how much to donate and to whom to donate? When we give coins to our church, is God more pleased when we do because we want to or because someone has told us we have to? Why does it make a difference?**

• Prayer •

God, You ask us to give to Your work. But we know we must give with a happy heart, not just because You tell us to. Help us to give to You and others with joy. Amen.

Lesson Twenty-Three

Leaving Judgment to God

• Activity •

Review with the children the excerpt from *The Life of Our Lord* in Lesson Twenty concerning the Pharisee and Mary of Bethany. Explain that Pharisees thought that keeping rules was important to please God. Ask the children to name some rules that adults think are important for children to keep. Record the list with a marker on a poster board or large sheet of paper. Then have them add to the list rules which teachers think are important for children to keep. Finally, have them add rules which just about everyone thinks are important to keep.

Let the children discuss and decide which of the rules on the poster board are also God's rules, as opposed to rules which people have created on their own. Circle God's rules with a different color of marker to make them stand out, and then discuss what makes God's rules different from people's rules.

• The Life of Our Lord •

One morning, [Jesus] was sitting in a place called the Mount of Olives, teaching the people who were all clustered round Him, listening and learning attentively, when a great noise was heard, and a crowd of Pharisees and some other people like them, called scribes, came running in with great cries and shouts, dragging among them a woman who had done wrong, and they all cried out together, "Master! Look at this woman. The law says she shall be pelted with stones until she is dead. But what say You? What say You?"

103

Jesus looked upon the noisy crowd attentively and knew that they had come to make Him say the law was wrong and cruel, and that if He said so, they would make it a charge against Him and would kill Him. They were ashamed and afraid as He looked into their faces, but they still cried out, "Come! What say You, Master? What say You?"

Jesus stooped down and wrote with His finger in the sand on the ground, "He that is without sin among you, let him throw the first stone at her." As they read this, looking over one another's shoulders, and as He repeated the words to them, they went away, one by one, ashamed, until not a man of all the noisy crowd was left there, and Jesus Christ and the woman, hiding her face in her hands, alone remained.

Then said Jesus Christ, "Woman, where are thine accusers? Hath no man condemned thee?" She answered, trembling, "No, Lord!" Then said our Savior, "Neither do I condemn thee. Go! And sin no more!" [Text: John 8:1-11]

Ask, **If someone had thrown a stone at the woman, would it then have been all right for someone else to throw a second stone or a third stone? What if someone had thrown only the last stone, after she was already hurt? What if the last stone had been just a pebble?**

• Another Thought •

Charles Dickens wrote a book titled *Hard Times*. In this book, Stephen Blackpool has a wife who spends much of her time away from home and most of her time drinking alcohol. Rachael, a friend to both Stephen and his wife, does not want Stephen to abandon his wife. She meets him and says:

"I have been here once before, today, Stephen. Landlady came round for me at dinnertime. There was someone here that needed looking to, she said. And 'deed she was right. All wandering and lost, Stephen. Wounded too, and bruised." He slowly moved to a chair and sat down, drooping his head before her.

"I came to do what little I could, Stephen; first, for that she worked with me when we were girls both, and for that you courted her and married her when I was her friend."

He laid his furrowed forehead on his hand, with a low groan.

"And next, for that I know your heart, and am right sure and certain that 'tis far too merciful to let her die, or even so much as suffer, for want of aid. Thou knowest who said, 'Let him who is without sin among you cast the first stone at her!' There have been plenty to do that. Thou art not the man to cast the last stone, Stephen, when she is brought so low."

Ask, **How have stones already been cast at Stephen's wife?** (Focus on the passage "All wandering and lost, Stephen. Wounded too, and bruised.") Ask, **Why is Rachael worried that Stephen might "cast the last stone" at his wife? Why should Stephen forgive and help his wife? Why does each one of us need Jesus' forgiveness just as much as anyone else does?**

• Prayer •

We are not perfect, God, and that is why You sent Jesus to forgive us. Remind us that we are no better than our brother or sister, and prevent us from ever judging someone else more harshly than we judge ourselves. Amen.

Lesson Twenty-Four

⌐ Helping Neighbors ⌐

• Activity •

Use the Lot Box to assign the children to groups of
three. Give each group a recent newspaper and scissors
and ask the teams to find a story in the newspaper about
someone who helped another person who was less fortunate. When a story is found, it should be cut out and
added to one poster board or large sheet of paper for later
display. Let the teams take turns telling everyone else
about their articles.

• The Life of Our Lord •

As our Savior sat teaching the people and answering
their questions, a certain lawyer stood up and said,
"Master, what shall I do that I may live again in happiness
after I am dead?" Jesus said to him, "The first of all the
commandments is, the Lord our God is one Lord, and
thou shalt love the Lord thy God with all thy heart, and
with all thy soul, and with all thy mind, and with all thy
strength. And the second is like unto it. Thou shalt love
thy neighbor as thyself. There is none other commandment greater than these."

Then the lawyer said, "But who is my neighbor? Tell
me, that I may know." Jesus answered in this parable:

"There was once a traveler," He said, "journeying
from Jerusalem to Jericho, who fell among thieves, and
they robbed him of his clothes and wounded him and
went away, leaving him half dead upon the road. A priest,
happening to pass that way while the poor man lay there,
saw him but took no notice and passed by on the other

side. Another man, a Levite, came that way and also saw him, but he only looked at him for a moment and then passed by, also. But a certain Samaritan who came traveling along that road no sooner saw him than he had compassion on him, and dressed his wounds with oil and wine, and set him on the beast he rode himself, and took him to an inn, and next morning took out of his pocket two pence and gave them to the landlord, saying, 'Take care of him, and whatever you may spend beyond this, in doing so, I will repay you when I come here again.' Now, which of these three men," said our Savior to the lawyer, "do you think should be called the neighbor of him who fell among the thieves?" The lawyer said, "The man who showed compassion on him." "True," replied our Savior. "Go thou and do likewise! Be compassionate to all men. For all men are your neighbors and brothers." [Text: Matthew 22:34-40; Mark 12:28-31; and Luke 10:25-37]

Ask, **Would people help those who are less fortunate if newspapers never reported the good deeds they did? Should we still respond to someone in need, even if no one but God will ever know about our good deed?**

• Another Thought •

We first met Toby Veck's daughter Meg and the orphan for whom Meg tried to be a mother in *The Chimes* in Lesson Twenty. Here, Toby is so deep in thought that Meg is unable to get his attention:

"Why! Lord!" said Toby. "The papers is full of obserwations as it is, and so's the Parliament. Here's last week's paper, now," taking a very dirty one from his pocket, and holding it from him at arm's length, "full of obserwations! Full of obserwations! I like to know the news as well as any man," said Toby, slowly, folding it a little smaller and putting it in his pocket again, "but it almost goes against the grain with me to read a paper now. It frightens me almost. I don't know what we poor people are coming to. Lord send we may be coming to something better in the New Year nigh upon us!"

"Why, father, father!" said a pleasant voice, hard by.

But Toby, not hearing it, continued to trot backwards and forwards, musing as he went and talking to himself.

"It seems as if we can't go right, or do right, or be righted," said Toby. "I hadn't much schooling, myself, when I was young, and I can't make out whether we have any business on the face of the earth, or not. Sometimes I think we must have—a little—and sometimes I think we must be intruding. I get so puzzled sometimes that I am not even able to make up my mind whether there is any good at all in us, or whether we are born bad. We seem to be dreadful things; we seem to give a deal of trouble; we are always being complained of and guarded against. One way or other, we fill the papers."

Ask, **Why does Toby think that being poor makes him a bad person? What would you tell Toby if you could meet him in person?**

• Prayer •

God, Your Word doesn't tell us to do good deeds when it is easy and we will get a lot of attention for it. You tell us to do good everywhere and anywhere we can, because by doing good we are sharing You with those in need. Help us to do good, God. Amen.

☞ The Importance of Prayer: Part Two ☜

• Activity •

Provide the children with construction paper, pencils, scissors and glue. Have each child sketch parts of a flower and cut them out. Then they should glue the parts together. Allow the children to make as many flowers as they like. Pin the flowers on a poster board or a large sheet of paper. Ask the children if there are enough flowers for a garden.

If they say "yes," ask, **Would there be enough flowers for a garden if one flower were removed? What if two flowers were removed? How about three flowers? At what point would there be not enough flowers? How do you know?** If they say "no," ask, **Would there be enough flowers for a garden if another flower were added? What if two flowers were added? How about three flowers? At what point would there be enough flowers? How do you know?**

Leave the flowers on display and tell the children to pretend that the flowers are from a garden Jesus visited, the garden of Gethsemane.

• The Life of Our Lord •

Jesus then led the way over a brook, called Cedron, into a garden that was called Gethsemane, and walked with three of the disciples into a retired part of the garden. Then He left them as He had left the others together, saying, "Wait here and watch!" and went away and prayed by Himself, while they, being weary, fell asleep.

And Christ suffered great sorrow and distress of mind

in His prayers in that garden, because of the wickedness of the men of Jerusalem who were going to kill Him, and He shed tears before God and was in deep and strong affliction. When His prayers were finished and He was comforted, He returned to the disciples and said, "Rise! Let us be going! He is close at hand, who will betray Me!" [Text Matthew 26:36-46; Mark 14:32-42; Luke 22:40-46; and John 18:1]

Ask, **Where did Jesus pray? What are some other places where people pray? Do we need to be in a special place in order to pray? Jesus knew that wicked men and one of His own disciples would work together to bring about His death — what, then, might Jesus have prayed to God in the Garden of Gethsemane? What kind of prayer is this? What other kinds of prayers can be prayed?** Tell each child to take his or her flower home to serve as a reminder of when Jesus prayed to God in the Garden of Gethsemane.

• Another Thought •

From a letter written by Charles Dickens to his youngest son, Edward, on the occasion of his leaving home for Australia:

I write this note today because your going away is much upon my mind, and because I want you to have a few parting words from me, to think of now and then at quiet times. I need not tell you that I love you dearly, and am very, very sorry in my heart to part with you. But this life is half made up of partings, and these pains must be borne.

It is my comfort and my sincere conviction that you are going to try the life for which you are best fitted...I therefore exhort you to persevere in a thorough determination to do whatever you have to do, as well as you can do it. I was not so old as you are now, when I first had to win my food, and to do it out of this determination, and I have never slackened in it since. Never take a mean advantage of anyone in any transaction, and never be hard upon people who are in your power. Try to do to others as you would have them do to you, and do not be discouraged if they fail sometimes. It is much better for you that they should fail in obeying the greatest rule laid down by our Savior than that you should. Never abandon the wholesome practice of saying your own private prayers night and morning. I have never abandoned it myself, and I know the comfort of it.

Tell the children that Charles Dickens, like any good father, wanted his child to lead a good life. Ask, **What advice did he give his son? Why did Dickens see prayer as an important part of leading a good life? Is prayer still important to us today? How important should it be in our lives?**

• Prayer •

God, You created prayer as a way we can talk to You anytime about anything. We also pray to hear Your guidance for our lives. We commit ourselves to praying to You as often and as honestly as we are able. Amen.

Lesson Twenty-Six

⌒ Sacredness ⌒

• Activity •

Provide markers or colored pencils and a roll of paper or poster boards attached together. Have the children make one mural that shows how their family (or families) spends Christmas Eve. Have each child explain his or her contribution to the mural. If space permits, put the mural on display.

• The Life of Our Lord •

The feast of the Passover now drawing very near, Jesus Christ, with His disciples, moved forward towards Jerusalem. When they were come near to that city, He pointed to a village and told two of His disciples to go there, and they would find an ass, with a colt, tied to a tree, which they were to bring to Him. Finding these animals exactly as Jesus had described, they brought them away, and Jesus, riding on the ass, entered Jerusalem. An immense crowd of people collected 'round Him as He went along, and throwing their robes on the ground, and cutting down green branches from the trees, and spreading them in His path, they shouted and cried, "Hosanna to the son of David!" (David had been a great king there.) "He comes in the name of the Lord! This is Jesus, the prophet of Nazareth!" And when Jesus went into the temple, He cast out the tables of the money changers, who wrongfully sat there, together with people who sold doves, saying, "My Father's House is a house of prayer, but ye have made it a den of thieves!" And when the people and children cried in the temple, "This is Jesus, the prophet of Nazareth," and would not be silenced, and when the blind and lame came flocking there in crowds and were healed by His hand, the chief priests and scribes and Pharisees were filled with fear and hatred of Him. But Jesus continued to heal the sick and to do good, and went and lodged at Bethany, a place that was very near the city of Jerusalem, but not within the walls. [Text: Matthew 21:1-17; Mark 11:1-10, 15-19; Luke 19:29-38, 45-48; and John 12:12-15].

Determine if the children know what a money changer does. If they do not know, ask, **What does it sound as if a money changer would do? Is there something wrong with being a money changer? If not, why was Jesus upset? Since Jesus makes it clear that church is not a place for buying and selling, what is church a place for?** Introduce the concept of sacredness. Then ask, **What makes a church sacred? How should we show God that a church is sacred through our behavior? Are Christmas and Christmas Eve sacred? How do we demonstrate this?**

• Another Thought •

Charles Dickens wrote in *A Christmas Carol*:

Once upon a time, of all the good days in the year, on Christmas Eve, old Scrooge sat busy in his counting house. It was cold, bleak, biting weather, foggy withal, and he could hear the people in the court outside go wheezing up and down, beating their hands upon their breasts and stamping their feet upon the pavement stones to warm them. The city clocks had only just gone three, but it was quite dark already—it had not been light all day—and candles were flaring in the windows of the neighboring offices, like ruddy smears upon the palpable brown air. The fog came pouring in at every chink and keyhole, and was so dense without, that although the court was of the narrowest, the houses opposite were mere phantoms.

Ask, **How was Scrooge spending Christmas Eve? How should he have been spending Christmas Eve?**

• Prayer •

God, we should always respect and enjoy Your church and our time in it. Help us to keep sacred our worship times and holidays. Amen.

✑ Acquiring and Keeping a Good Name ✑

• Activity •

Play a game in which each child takes a turn calling out a first name that begins with each letter of the alphabet. Omit the children's names—their names were part of the activity in Lesson One. Record each name on a poster board or large sheet of paper. After the letter "Z" has been reached, look up in the name book the meaning of each name. Add each meaning next to each name on the poster board. Finally, have the children identify which names seem to have a happy meaning and which seem to have a sad meaning.

• The Life of Our Lord •

Now Judas knew that garden well, for our Savior had often walked there with His disciples, and…[Judas] came there, accompanied by a strong guard of men and officers, which had been sent by the chief priests and Pharisees. It being dark, they carried lanterns and torches. They were armed with swords and staves, too, for they did not know but that the people would rise and defend Jesus Christ, and this had made them afraid to seize Him boldly in the day, when He sat teaching the people.

As the leader of this guard had never seen Jesus Christ and did not know Him from the apostles, Judas had said to them, "The man whom I kiss will be He." As he advanced to give this wicked kiss, Jesus said to the soldiers, "Whom do you seek?" "Jesus of Nazareth," they answered. "Then," said our Savior, "I am He. Let My disciples here go freely. I am He." Which Judas confirmed by saying, "Hail, Master!" and kissing Him. Whereupon

Jesus said, "Judas, thou betrayest Me with a kiss!"

The guard then ran forward to seize Him. No one offered to protect Him, except Peter, who, having a sword, drew it and cut off the right ear of the high priest's servant, who was one of them and whose name was Malchus. But Jesus made Him sheathe his sword, and gave Himself up. Then, all the disciples forsook Him and fled, and there remained not one—not one to bear Him company. [Text: Matthew 26:47-56; Mark 14:43-50; Luke 22:47-53; and John 18:2-12]

Look up the name "Judas" in the name book. If it is there, tell the children what it means. If it is not, ask, **What does the absence of Judas from the book suggest? Why is the name not favored by Christians? What makes a name good or bad—what the name means or how the person with the name treats others?**

• Another Thought •

Dickens wrote a book titled *A Tale of Two Cities*. Early in the book, a bad man pretends to be named John Barsad and he tells lies in the court of law, hoping to have an innocent man put to death for treason. The innocent man's lawyer, Mr. Stryver, explains to the jury how:

Barsad was a hired spy and traitor, an unblushing trafficker in blood, and one of the greatest scoundrels upon earth since accursed Judas—which he certainly did look rather like.

Ask, **What did Judas do to lose his good name? What is Dickens telling us about Barsad when the lawyer Stryver compares him to Judas?**

• Prayer •

God, no one on earth may remember our actions, but You do. Guide us so that people know we are Yours. Amen.

Lesson Twenty-Eight

Jesus' Crucifixion

• Activity •

Ask, **What different meanings does the word "cross" have?** Answers should include the wooden structure on which Jesus was crucified and symbols of that structure; answers may also include any figure made by two straight lines which meet at their midpoints, a place to go from one side of the road to the other, a dog with parents of two different breeds, and verbs telling either of physical movement or of going against another person's plans. Ask, **Why is the Christian cross the most important meaning of the word "cross"? What did Jesus do for us by dying upon the cross? What should we think of when we see a symbol of Jesus' cross?**

Give each child a ruler, a pencil, a sheet of construction paper and scissors to draw and cut out a Christian cross.

• The Life of Our Lord •

That you may know what the people meant when they said, "Crucify Him!" I must tell you that in those times, which were very cruel times indeed—let us thank God and Jesus Christ that they are past!—it was the custom to kill people who were sentenced to death by nailing them alive on a great wooden cross, planted upright in the ground, and leaving them there, exposed to the sun and wind, and day and night, until they died of pain and thirst. It was the custom, too, to make them walk to the place of execution, carrying the crosspiece of wood to which their hands were to be afterwards nailed, that their shame and suffering might be the greater.

Bearing His cross upon His shoulder like the commonest and most wicked criminal, our blessed Savior, Jesus Christ, surrounded by the persecuting crowd, went out of Jerusalem to a place called in the Hebrew language Golgotha, that is, the place of a skull. And being come to a hill called Mount Calvary, they hammered cruel nails through His hands and feet and nailed Him on the cross, between two other crosses, on each of which a common thief was nailed in agony. Over His head they fastened this writing: "Jesus of Nazareth, the King of the Jews," in three languages: in Hebrew, in Greek, and in Latin.

Meantime, a guard of four soldiers, sitting on the ground, divided His clothes (which they had taken off) into four parcels for themselves, and cast lots for His coat and sat there, gambling and talking, while He suffered. They offered Him vinegar to drink, mixed with gall; and wine, mixed with myrrh; but He took none. And the wicked people who passed that way mocked Him and said, "If Thou be the Son of God, come down from the cross." The chief priests also mocked Him and said, "He came to save sinners. Let Him save Himself!" One of the thieves, too, railed at him in His torture and said, "If Thou be Christ, save Thyself and us." But the other thief, who was penitent, said, "Lord! Remember me when Thou comest into Thy kingdom!" And Jesus answered, "Today, thou shalt be with Me in paradise."

None were there to take pity on Him, but one disciple and four women. God bless those women for their true and tender hearts! They were the mother of Jesus, His mother's sister, Mary the wife of Cleophas, and Mary Magdalene. The disciple was he whom Jesus loved, John, who had leaned upon His breast and asked Him which was the betrayer.

When Jesus saw them standing at the foot of the cross, He said to His mother that John would be her son, to comfort her when He was dead, and from that hour John was as a son to her and loved her.

At about the sixth hour, a deep and terrible darkness came over all the land and lasted until the ninth hour, when Jesus cried out with a loud voice, "My God, My God, why hast Thou forsaken Me!" The soldiers, hearing Him, dipped a sponge in some vinegar, that was standing there, and fastening it to a long reed, put it up to His mouth. When He had received it, He said, "It is finished!" And crying, "Father! Into Thy hands I commend My spirit!" died.

Then, there was a dreadful earthquake, and the great wall of the temple cracked, and the rocks were rent asunder. The guards, terrified at these sights, said to each other, "Surely this was the Son of God!" And the people who had been watching the cross from a distance (among whom were many women) smote upon their breasts and went, fearfully and sadly, home.

The next day, being the Sabbath, the Jews were anxious that the bodies should be taken down at once, and made that request to Pilate. Therefore some soldiers came and broke the legs of the two criminals to kill them, but coming to Jesus and finding Him already dead, they only pierced his side with a spear. From the wound, there came out blood and water. [Text: Matthew 27:33-56; Mark 15:22-41; Luke 23:33-49; and John 19:17-20, 23-27, and 29-34]

Ask, **Have you learned anything from this reading about Jesus' crucifixion that you did not know or did not remember? What was it?** Review Dickens' comment that part of the purpose of crucifixion is so "shame and suffering might be the greater." Then ask, **If Dickens is**

correct, then why do we display crosses in churches? What did death on a cross mean before Jesus Himself was crucified? What does a cross now mean to Christians? Tell each child to take his or her cross home to serve as a reminder of the pain Jesus had to endure for the sake of our sins.

• Another Thought •

Another of Charles Dickens books is *The Haunted Man*. This book tells the story of Mr. Redlaw, a man with painful memories who is granted his wish of not having to live with any memories at all. He learns his lesson that memories are important to us all, and when his memory is restored, he prays:

[Milly's] quiet voice was quieter than ever, as she took her husband's arm and laid her head against it.

"Children love me so, that sometimes I half fancy—it's a silly fancy, William —they have some way I don't know of, of feeling for my little child, and me, and understanding why their love is precious to me. If I have been quiet since, I have been more happy, William, in a hundred ways. Not least happy, dear, in this—that even when my little child was born and dead but a few days and I was weak and sorrowful, and could not help grieving a little, the thought arose, that if I tried to lead a good life, I should meet in heaven a bright creature, who would call me Mother!" [Hearing Milly say this to her husband,] Redlaw fell upon his knees, with a loud cry.

"O Thou," he said, "who through the teaching of pure love, has graciously restored me to the memory which was the memory of Christ upon the cross, and of all the good who perished in His cause, receive my thanks, and bless her!"

Ask, **What is it that Mr. Redlaw is most thankful to**

be able to remember again? Why is his knowledge of Jesus on the cross so important to him? What would his life be like if he had never known about Jesus? What would our lives be like if we had never known about Jesus?

• Prayer •

God, we are so sorrowful that Jesus had to endure pain for the sake of our sins. We are reminded of His act every time we see a cross. Thank You for the clean life we are able to have because You sent Your Son for us. Amen.

Jesus' Resurrection

• Activity •

Draw the name of a child from the Lot Box and give that child an empty shoe box with a lid. While the other children keep their eyes closed, the selected child should hide something in the box. Then have everyone take a turn asking a yes/no question about what is hidden in the box. Each time the answer is "yes," the child who asked the question is entitled to one guess about what is in the box. Limit the number of questions to ten. If a child's guess is correct, that child hides the next item in the box. If the hidden object is not guessed, everyone gets to see it. Then, draw the name of another child from the Lot Box in order to continue the game.

Reserve enough time so that you are the last person to hide something in the box; however, keep the box empty and answer the children's questions on the basis that the box contains the answer "nothing." When the correct answer is guessed or given, explain that "nothing" is what Jesus' tomb contained when Mary Magdalene, another Mary, and other women first looked inside it after Jesus' resurrection.

• The Life of Our Lord •

There was a good man named Joseph of Arimathea (a Jewish city), who believed in Christ, and going to Pilate privately, for fear of the Jews, begged that he might have the body. Pilate consenting, he and one Nicodemus rolled it in linen and spices (it was the custom of the Jews to prepare bodies for burial in that way) and buried it in a new tomb or sepulcher, which had been cut out of a rock in a garden near to the place of crucifixion, and where no one had ever yet been buried. They then rolled a great stone to the mouth of the sepulcher and left Mary Magdalene and the other Mary sitting there, watching it.

The chief priests and Pharisees, remembering that Jesus Christ had said to His disciples that He would rise from the grave on the third day after His death, went to Pilate and prayed that the sepulcher might be well taken care of until that day, lest the disciples should steal the body and afterwards say to the people that Christ was risen from the dead. Pilate agreeing to this, a guard of soldiers was set over it constantly, and the stone was sealed up besides. And so it remained, watched and sealed, until the third day, which was the first day of the week.

When that morning began to dawn, Mary Magdalene and the other Mary and some other women came to the sepulcher, with some more spices which they had prepared. As they were saying to each other, "How shall we roll away the stone?" the earth trembled and shook, and an angel, descending from heaven, rolled it back and then sat resting on it. His countenance was like lightning, and his garments were white as snow, and at sight of him, the men of the guard fainted away with fear, as if they were dead.

Mary Magdalene saw the stone rolled away, and waiting to see no more, ran to Peter and John, who were coming towards the place, and said, "They have taken away the Lord, and we know not where they have laid Him!" They immediately ran to the tomb, but John, being the faster of the two, outran the other and got there first. He stooped down and looked in and saw the linen

clothes in which the body had been wrapped, lying there, but he did not go in. When Peter came up, he went in and saw the linen clothes lying in one place and a napkin that had been bound about the head in another. John also went in then and saw the same things. Then they went home to tell the rest.

But Mary Magdalene remained outside the sepulcher, weeping. After a little time, she stooped down and looked in and saw two angels, clothed in white, sitting where the body of Christ had lain. These said to her, "Woman, why weepest thou?" She answered, "Because they have taken away my Lord, and I know not where they have laid Him." As she gave this answer, she turned round and saw Jesus standing behind her, but did not then know Him.

"Woman," said He, "why weepest thou? What seekest thou?" She, supposing Him to be the gardener, replied, "Sir! If thou hast borne my Lord hence, tell me where thou hast laid Him, and I will take Him away." Jesus pronounced her name, "Mary." Then she knew Him, and, starting, exclaimed, "Master!" "Touch me not," said Christ, "for I am not yet ascended to My Father, but go to My disciples, and say unto them, I ascend unto My Father and your Father, and to My God and to your God!"

Accordingly, Mary Magdalene went and told the disciples that she had seen Christ and what He had said to her, and with them she found the other women whom she had left at the sepulcher when she had gone to call those two disciples Peter and John. These women told her and the rest that they had seen at the tomb two men in shining garments, at sight of whom they had been afraid and had bent down, but who had told them that the Lord was risen; and also that as they came to tell this, they had seen Christ, on the way, and had held Him by the feet and worshipped

Him. But these accounts seemed to the apostles at that time as idle tales, and they did not believe them.

The soldiers of the guard, too, when they recovered from their fainting fit and went to the chief priests to tell them what they had seen, were silenced with large sums of money and were told by them to say that the disciples had stolen the body away while they were asleep. [Text: Matthew 27:57-66 and 28:1-15; Mark 15:43-47 and 16:1-11; Luke 23:50-56 and 24:1-12; and John 19:38-42 and 20:1-18]

Review who had wanted to find Jesus' body in His tomb. Then ask, **Why did they want to find Jesus' body? Why should they have been happy when they learned that the tomb was empty? Why were they not happy at first?**

• Another Thought •

We first met the seven poor travelers in Lesson Five and then learned more about one of them in Lesson Fifteen. Here, the latter traveler tells more about his walk on Christmas Day:

Going through the woods, the softness of my tread upon the mossy ground and among the brown leaves enhanced the Christmas sacredness by which I felt surrounded. As the whitened stems environed me, I thought how the Founder of the time had never raised His benignant hand, save to bless and heal, except in the case of one unconscious tree. By Cobham Hall, I came to the village, and the churchyard where the dead had been quietly buried, "in the sure and certain hope" which Christmas-time inspired. What children could I see at play, and not be loving of, recalling who had loved them! No garden that I passed was out of unison with the day, for I remembered that the tomb was in a garden, and that "she, supposing Him to be the gardener," had said, "Sir, if thou have borne Him hence, tell me were thou hast laid Him, and I will take Him away."

Ask, **What is the name of the holy day on which Mary Magdalene met Jesus and thought He was the gardener? How is it that the tomb and garden of Easter also make Charles Dickens think of Christmas?**

• Prayer •

What a surprise that must have been when Jesus' friends found an empty tomb! God, Jesus followed Your plan even when He knew He would suffer pain. But we see why Your plan was right, and we love You for it.

Lesson Thirty

～ Overcoming Doubt ～

• Activity •

Before the children arrive, remove everything on display from other activities and keep it all out of sight. As the children gather, give them a minute or two to notice and comment on the empty display area. If no one notices and comments, ask the children what is different about the room. Once they are aware, ask, **What would you tell someone who had never seen what was on display, but who wanted to know? What if that person did not believe you? What if that person claimed that there was never anything on display, and that what you are saying is not true? How would you prove to someone what was there? What if you could not find what was there to show the person as proof?**

• The Life of Our Lord •

While they were speaking, Jesus suddenly stood in the midst of all the company and said, "Peace be unto ye!" Seeing that they were greatly frightened, He showed them His hands and feet and invited them to touch Him, and, to encourage them and give them time to recover themselves, He ate a piece of broiled fish and a piece of honeycomb before them all.

But Thomas, one of the twelve apostles, was not there at that time, and when the rest said to him afterwards, "We have seen the Lord!" he answered, "Except I shall see in His hands the print of the nails and thrust my hand into His side, I will not believe!" At that moment, though the doors were all shut, Jesus again appeared, standing among them, and said, "Peace be unto you!" Then He said to Thomas, "Reach hither thy finger and behold My hands, and reach hither thy hand, and thrust it into My side, and be not faithless, but believing." And Thomas answered and said to Him, "My Lord and my God!" Then said Jesus, "Thomas, because thou hast seen Me, thou hast believed. Blessed are they that have not seen Me, and yet have believed." [Text: Luke 24:36-43; John 20:19-20, 24-29]

Ask, **Why did Thomas not believe the other apostles when they told him that they had seen Jesus risen from the dead? What kind of proof did Thomas demand? Was Thomas given the proof that he insisted upon? Who gave it to him? What writings does God want us to accept as proof of His words for us?**

• Another Thought •

We have already met the characters Stephen Blackpool, his wife and their friend Rachael from *Hard Times* in Lesson Twenty-Three. Here, we meet Louisa Gradgrind and her father, Thomas Gradgrind. After years of keeping her unhappiness hidden from her father, she finally confides in him. He then tells her:

"I never knew you were unhappy, my child."

"Father, I always knew it. In this strife I have almost repulsed and crushed my better angel into a demon. What I have learned has left me doubting, misbelieving, despising, regretting, what I have not learned."

Ask, **Is Louisa wise to confide in her father about her doubts that have led to her unhappiness with her life?** Say, **Louisa knows there is much that she has not learned. What might her father be able to do to help her? To whom can we turn whenever we have doubts**

that we need to overcome? How can our parents help? How can God help?

• Prayer •

God, You tell us in the Bible that we have no reason to doubt You. Help us to live a life of faith, Lord. Amen.

~ **Baptism** ~

• Activity •

Distribute to every child a paper towel and a paper cup half-full of water. Make available assorted food coloring that can be dispensed in drops, and tell the children that their goal is to create a cup of water with a color which is different from everyone else's. Each child must keep his or her color a secret by not letting others see the drops he or she adds to the water, and by keeping the cup covered with a piece of paper towel. After everyone has created a color, inspect the results and announce who has succeeded in creating a color that no one else has. If there are any duplicate colors, have the children with the duplicate colors take another turn and add one or more additional drops of color to their cups. Continue to identify unique colors until every child has succeeded or the remaining colors are so dark as to make the creation of any further variations difficult.

• The Life of Our Lord •

When Christ was seen no more, the apostles began to teach the people as He had commanded them. And having chosen a new apostle, named Matthias, to replace the wicked Judas, they wandered into all countries, telling the people of Christ's life and death, and of His crucifixion and resurrection, and of the lessons He had taught, and baptizing them in Christ's name. And through the power He had given them, they healed the sick, and gave sight to the blind, and speech to the dumb, and hearing to the deaf, as He had done. And Peter, being thrown into prison, was delivered from it in the dead of night by an angel, and once, his words before God caused a man named Ananias and his wife, Sapphira, who had told a lie, to be struck down dead upon the earth. [Text: Acts 1:15-26; 5:1-11, 17-20; and 12:3-11]

Ask, **What color is water that comes out of a faucet? What makes river water seem brown? What makes lake water seem blue?** Have the children count how many differnt colors of water they made. Ask, **With so many possible colors of water, why does the water's color have nothing to do with one's baptism? What is truly important about baptism?**

• Another Thought •

Charles Dickens wrote to Mrs. John Leech:

Dora is very ill, with something like congestion of the brain. She was taken with it on Saturday at midnight, and though better this morning, is not out of danger [and was] baptized by [Rev.] White, who was dining here.

Tell the children that Dickens was quite right about Dora's illness, that her ill health prevented her from traveling to church to receive her baptism. Ask, **When it is time for our baptism, do we have to be in a church to receive it? Do you know where members of your family were baptized? In what river did John baptize Jesus?**

• Prayer •

God, thank You for the act of baptism that allows us to cleanse ourselves of sin. We know that baptism is very special and a part of Your plan for us. We are so glad to be Your children. Amen.

Lesson Thirty-Two

⌒ Offering Thanksgiving ⌒

• Activity •

Give each child two sheets of writing paper, two envelopes and a pencil. Have the children use the first sheet to write a letter of thankfulness to someone as a surprise. Encourage them to promise to address and mail (or deliver) the letter later. They should use the second sheet to thank God for anything for which they want to show gratitude. Instruct them to place this sheet in the second envelope and to open the envelope at bedtime and read the letter as a private prayer of thanksgiving.

• The Life of Our Lord •

Remember! It is Christianity to do good always, even to those who do evil to us. It is Christianity to love our neighbors as ourselves, and to do to all men as we would have them do to us. It is Christianity to be gentle, merciful, and forgiving, and to keep those qualities quiet in our own hearts, and never make a boast of them, or of our prayers, or of our love of God, but always to show that we love Him by humbly trying to do right in everything. If we do this and remember the life and lessons of our Lord Jesus Christ and try to act up to them, we may confidently hope that God will forgive us our sins and mistakes, and enable us to live and die in peace.

Ask, **Which good behaviors did Charles Dickens name in this part of *The Life of Our Lord*?** The list should include:

1. Do good always.

2. Love one's neighbor as oneself.

3. Do to others as we would have them do to us.

4. Be gentle.

5. Be merciful.

6. Be forgiving.

7. Do not boast of being good.

8. Pray to God.

9. Love God.

10. Be humble.

11. Try to do what is right, according to God.

12. Remember Jesus' life.

13. Remember Jesus' teachings.

14. Ask God to forgive our sins and mistakes.

• Another Thought •

Ask, **What would Charles Dickens have written to his children if he had known that he would never see them again and could write only one letter?** Then read aloud the letter below, which Dickens wrote to his son Alfred in Australia just twenty days before Dickens died. Tell the children that Alfred received the letter in the mail after he had already learned by telegraph that his father had died.

My dear Alfred,

I have just time to tell you under my own hand that I invited Mr. Bear to a dinner of such guests as he would naturally like to see, and that we took to him very much and got on with him capitally.

I am doubtful whether Plorn [Dickens' son Edward] is taking to Australia. Can you find out his real mind? I notice that he always writes as if his present life were the be-all and the end-all of his emigration, and as if I had no idea of you two becoming proprietors and aspiring to the first positions in the colony, without casting off the old connection.

From Mr. Bear I had the best accounts of you. I told him that they did not surprise me, for I had unbounded faith in you. For which take my love and blessing.

They will have told you all the news here, and that I am hard at work. This is not a letter so much as an assurance that I never think of you without hope and comfort.

—Ever, my dear Alfred, your affectionate Father

Ask, **Do you think Charles Dickens would have been pleased to have known that these were his final words to his son? Why?** Remind the children that they have two very important letters of their own to deliver.

• Prayer •

God, we have learned that we should always be thankful and live as Your disciples because we never know when we might be leading someone to You. We love You and thank You that You guide our lives. Amen.

⌒ Appendix ⌒

In order to learn in what ways children might respond to hearing Dickens' children's New Testament read aloud, I undertook my own reading with my then six-year-old daughter, Emily. Immediately after each reading, I recorded every verbal interaction she had initiated. Even though I knew that my readings would be unlike Dickens' (in that I had not read to her many times the excerpts contained in *The Dickens Family Gospel* study guides), I expected some of this disadvantage to be offset by Emily's regular attendance in Sunday school since the age of four. I also knew that I would not be able to supplement the text with Dickens' comments and questions, there being no record of these. Accordingly, I decided to refrain from making any comments or asking any questions at all, in order to capture fully my daughter's self-initiated comments and questions. I did, however, answer her questions as they were asked, both because Dickens would have done the same with his children and because I wanted to maintain her willingness to ask questions.

Responses

Lesson One: The Importance of Knowing Jesus

Dickens begins the lesson, "My dear children, I am very anxious that you should know something about the history of Jesus Christ." Emily immediately wanted to know just how many children Dickens had (at the time, six). Then she wanted to know if there would be any pictures for her to see. I showed her a facsimile of the first page of Dickens' original manuscript, on which he had written the words which I had just read aloud. She asked why some words had been crossed out, so I simply said that he wrote in ink and was not able to erase any mistakes. She noticed that Dickens spelled the word "show" s-h-e-w and wanted to know if that was a word he should have crossed out and spelled correctly.

I began to worry that my reading aloud in the absence of my own commentary and questioning would merely promote more such responses, interesting but not substantive in terms of the study guide's content.

Lesson Five: Praising God Through Song

It was not until Lesson Five that Emily responded to another part of the excerpted text. The passage reads:

"So Joseph and Mary and her son Jesus Christ (who are commonly called The Holy Family) traveled towards Jerusalem, but hearing on the way that King Herod's son was the new king, and fearing that he, too, might want to hurt the child, they turned out of the way and went to live in Nazareth."

Emily asked what "Nazareth" is, not interpreting the sentence as naming a place.

Lesson Six: The Importance of Prayer (Part One)

When Emily heard that Joseph and Mary "thought He was somewhere among the people, though they did not see Him," she announced that Jesus was in the Temple, teaching others about God. As Dickens explains: "They found Him sitting in the Temple, talking about the goodness of God and how we should all pray to Him, with some learned men who were called doctors. They were not what you understand by the word 'doctors' now; they did not attend sick people. They were scholars and clever men."

Here, Emily said that Dickens should not have used the word "now" about the meaning of the word "doctors," because her daddy was going to be one (I was working on my Ph.D. at the time).

Lesson Seven: Promises (Part One)

When Emily heard that "[t]here was a river, not very far from Jerusalem, called the River Jordan, and in this water John baptized those people who would come to him and promise to be better," she wanted to know if John's baptizing people made them be better people.

Lesson Eight: Promises (Part Two)

Emily listened intently to Dickens' account of John the Baptist's death and then simply observed that Jesus could have brought him back to life.

Lesson Nine: Charity

Emily was reminded of the story of Cinderella when she heard Dickens' comment about the garments of the poor: "These twelve are called the apostles or disciples, and He chose them from among poor men in order that the poor might know always after that, in all years to come, that Heaven was made for them as well as for the rich, and that God makes no difference between those who wear good clothes and those who go barefoot and in rags."

Lesson Eleven: Humility (Part One)

Emily heard Dickens' address his children: "[Jesus] taught His disciples in these stories, because He knew the people liked to hear them and would remember what He said better, if He said it in that way. They are called 'parables,' the parables of our Savior, and I wish you to remember that word, as I shall soon have some more of these parables to tell you about."

She told me that another parable is about the lost sheep and explained that we are like the sheep and Jesus is the shepherd.

Something in the parable of the Pharisee and the publican caused her to associate it with one of her friends. Dickens recounts: "And among other parables, Christ said to these same Pharisees, because of their pride, that two men once went up into the Temple to pray, of whom one was a Pharisee and one a publican. The Pharisee said, 'God, I thank Thee, that I am not unjust as other men are or bad as this publican is!' The publican, standing afar off, would not lift up his eyes to Heaven, but struck his breast and only said, 'God, be merciful to me, a sinner!' And God, our Savior told them, would be merciful to that man rather than the other and would be better pleased with his prayer, because he made it with a humble and a lowly heart."

At this point, Emily told me that her friend and her friend's mother do not go to church, but they should, in order to worship God.

Lesson Fourteen: Miracles (Part One)

Emily responded to the following passage in Lesson Fourteen: "When [Jesus] came out of the Wilderness, He began to cure sick people by only laying His hand upon them, for God had given Him power to heal the sick, and to give sight to the blind, and to do many wonderful and solemn things of which I shall tell you more by and by and which are called the miracles of Christ."

Emily asked if the first miracle would be Jesus' feeding others. Told no, she said it must be turning water into wine.

Lesson Fifteen: Miracles (Part Two)

Emily said that she remembered about all the fish that were caught after Jesus said, "Let down the net again." She was most interested in the little girl who had died, and she wanted to know if she really came back to life. I told her yes, and she stated that the girl must have come back to life because Jesus is so good and because He is God's son.

Lesson Sixteen: Miracles (Part Three)

When Emily heard about "a dreadful madman who lived among the tombs," she wanted to know what the word "madman" means. After I explained the meaning, she told me about a story she had seen on television in which a man only pretended to be mad. After hearing of the feeding of the five thousand, she said that Jesus was the only one there who knew how to make more food.

Lesson Eighteen: Forgiveness (Part One)

During the parable of the wicked servant, Emily identified as part of the Lord's Prayer "how can you expect God to forgive you, if you do not forgive others," right before she heard Dickens' comment, "This is the meaning of that part of the Lord's Prayer where we say, 'Forgive us our trespasses…'"

Lesson Nineteen: Compassion

In Lesson Nineteen, Dickens tells how Jesus commanded Lazarus "in a loud and solemn voice" to come forth from his grave. He continues: "At this sight, so awful and affecting, many of the people there believed that Christ was indeed the Son of God, come to instruct and save mankind. But others ran to tell the Pharisees, and from that day the Pharisees resolved among themselves—to prevent more people from believing in Him—that Jesus should be killed. And they agreed among themselves, meeting in the Temple for that purpose, that if He came into Jerusalem before the Feast of the Passover, which was then approaching, He should be seized." The only word Emily questioned for meaning was "seized."

Lesson Twenty-Three: Leaving Judgment to God

This lesson contains the account of the woman caught in adultery, although Dickens does not use that term. Rather, he has the scribes and Pharisees cry out to Jesus that the woman had done wrong. When Emily heard that Jesus wrote, "He that is without sin among you, let him throw the first stone at her," she wanted to know why only one stone was supposed to be thrown. When I reached the end of the account, Emily said that Jesus wants the woman to be good, even though only Jesus is always good.

Lesson Twenty-Four: Helping Neighbors

Emily recognized the parable of the Good Samaritan and said that it would be about the hurt man who was helped by another man. She added that she learned about the Good Samaritan at summer Bible camp.

Lesson Twenty-Eight: Jesus' Crucifixion

Before recounting the crucifixion, Dickens explains: "That you may know what the people meant when they said, 'Crucify Him!' I must tell you that in those times, which were very cruel times indeed (let us thank God and Jesus Christ that they are past!) it was the custom to kill people who were sentenced to death by nailing them alive on a great wooden cross, planted upright in the ground and leaving them there, exposed to the sun and wind, and day and night, until they died of pain and thirst."

Emily told me that she knew just what Jesus looked like on a cross, because she has seen it in church.

Lesson Twenty-Nine: Jesus' Resurrection

When Emily heard of Jesus' resurrection, she said she knew that people would touch Jesus' hands.

Findings

Emily's responses to the text contained in the lessons suggest three general categories of responses that any child can be expected to make.

First, even with Dickens' simplified language, Emily still asked some questions about vocabulary. The answers to such questions lend themselves to a discussion of the significance of those words. Even with a child who does not take it upon himself or herself to ask about words which are unclear, a parent or teacher can initiate vocabulary questions and discussion by carefully observing the child's face for signs of puzzlement during the oral presentation.

Second, Emily commented on what she had already learned about Jesus' life and teachings, both from the standpoint of what Dickens told and what she expected him later to tell. For a child who already has some scriptural knowledge, when such comments are made, it is an ideal time to correct misunderstandings and to expand upon the child's foundational knowledge. For instance, it was necessary for me to explain to Emily that Jesus was not calling for someone to throw just one stone, as opposed to many stones, at the woman, rather that Jesus knew that no one was justified in throwing any stones at all. I might then have gone on to explain that the men were not even interested in the woman's deeds, but instead were merely using her in order to try to trap Jesus into saying something which they could then use against Him. Even with a child who has not yet learned much Scripture, after several readings of Dickens' text, I would expect comments like Emily's to begin to be made, since the comments could then be based on a growing familiarity with that text.

Third, Emily shared associations she made on her own between something in Dickens' writings and in other knowledge or experience she had. The key to eliciting such responses must necessarily be reading the text aloud as

Dickens did, while maintaining an environment in which any interruptions for questions and comments are encouraged and welcomed. While a child's associations with other knowledge and experience can scarcely be anticipated, when they occur they can certainly be worthy of exploration. In Emily's case, the parallel she drew between the apostles' clothes and Cinderella's clothes could lead to further comparisons, perhaps culminating with Jesus' observation that it is not what one eats which matters but rather what comes out of one's mouth. In the instance of Emily's concern that her friend and her friend's mother did not go to church, we shortly thereafter invited them to join us in church.

I can find no reason to assert either that the responses of Dickens' children would have lent themselves to significantly different categories, or that the responses of any children should lend themselves to significantly different categories. Rather, I suggest that specific responses within the above three categories vary based on personal knowledge and experience. Dickens' New Testament, derived as closely as it is from the King James Bible, is sound. His pedagogy proves equally sound.

☞ Bibliography ☜

Blathwayt, Raymond. (1910, November 12). "Reminiscences of Dickens: An Interview with Mr. Alfred Tennyson Dickens." *Great Thoughts from Master Minds*, pp. 104-105.

Dickens, Charles. (1991). *Bleak House*. Oxford: Oxford University Press.

———. (1991). *Christmas Books*. Oxford: Oxford University Press.

———. (1991). *Christmas Stories*. Oxford: Oxford University Press.

———. (1991). *Dombey and Son*. Oxford: Oxford University Press.

———. (1992). *Great Expectations*. Oxford: Oxford University Press.

———. (1991). *Hard Times*. Oxford: Oxford University Press.

———. (1934). *The Life of Our Lord*. New York: Simon and Schuster.

———. (1989). *Oliver Twist*. Oxford: Oxford University Press.

———. (1991). *A Tale of Two Cities*. Oxford: Oxford University Press.

Dickens, Mamie. (1885, January). "Charles Dickens at Home." *The Cornhill Magazine*, pp. 32-51.

Egan, Madonna. (1983). *Telling "The Blessed History": Charles Dickens's "The Life of Our Lord"* (Volumes I and II). Doctoral dissertation, University of Minnesota.

Forster, John. (1872-1874). *The Life of Charles Dickens* (Volumes I-III). London: Chapman and Hall.

Hogarth, Georgiana; Dickens, Mamie; and Hutton, Laurence (Eds.). (1903). *The Works of Charles Dickens: Letters and Speeches*. New York: Hearst's International Library.

"Letters to John Leech." (1938, Autumn). *The Dickensian*, pp. 225-231.

Osborne, Charles C. (Ed.). (1932). *Letters of Charles Dickens to the Baroness Burdett-Coutts*. New York: E.P. Dutton & Co., Inc.

About the Author

Robert Conrad Hanna began his teaching career at Lake Forest Academy-Ferry Hall in Illinois, after earning a bachelor of arts degree in English literature from Lake Forest College and a master's degree from Northwestern University. While working on an educational specialist degree at the College of William and Mary, he taught at St. Margaret's School in Virginia. He pursued the doctor of philosophy degree in curriculum and teaching at the University of North Carolina, during which time he taught at Gaston Day School and Belmont Abbey College. After receiving his Ph.D., he accepted the position of assistant professor of education at Hillsdale College, where he now serves as chairman of teacher education.

Dr. Hanna recently returned from London, where he completed the annotated bibliography of Charles Dickens' *The Life of Our Lord* for the Garland Dickens bibliographies. He is editor of the *Journal of the Midwest History of Education Society*, and serves as the Society's president. His articles have appeared in *The Dickensian, English Journal, Illinois Schools Journal, Imprimis, Kappa Delta Pi Record, Resources in Education, Safety & Health,* and *Virginia English Bulletin*. He has been recognized by the education honorary societies Kappa Phi Kappa, Kappa Delta Pi, and Kappa Delta Epsilon for his commitment to the moral education of children.

Dr. Hanna and his wife, Lesley, reside in Hillsdale, Michigan, with their daughters Charlotte, 15, and Emily, 8. They attend St. Peter's Episcopal Church in Hillsdale.